# Traveling History among the Ghosts

## *A Road Tripper's Guide to Abandoned Places in the Red River Valley*

**Robin Cole-Jett**
**Red River Historian**

Traveling History among the Ghosts: Abandoned Places in the Red River Valley

ISBN: 978-0-578-4997-6

Library of Congress Control Number: 2019904572

Printed in the United States of America

Red River Historian Press
Lewisville, TX 75077

Visit Red River Historian Press at www.redriverhistorian.com

Publisher's Cataloging-in Publication

Cole-Jett, Robin.
    Traveling History among the Ghosts: Abandoned Places in the Red River Valley / by Robin Cole-Jett.
        p. cm.
        Includes index.
        LCCN: 2019904572
        ISBN: 978057849976

# Traveling History among the Ghosts: A Road Tripper's Guide to Abandoned Places in the Red River Valley

## Table of Contents

Table of Photographs      5

Acknowledgements and Dedication      10

Ghost Town Hunting in the Red River Valley      11

Part One      14
*What makes a Ghost Town?*      15
*A Short History of Red River Settlement*      18

Part Two      52
*Louisiana Ghost Towns*      54
         Meeker, Moorehead, Cloutierville, Derry /
         Magnolia, Melrose, St. Matthew, Bermuda /
         Oakland, Grand Ecore, Powhatan, Hanna,
         Caspiana, Gloster, Keachi, Taylortown,
         Mayers, Belcher, Hosston, Mira, Rodessa
*Arkansas Ghost Towns*      87
         Doddridge, Rondo, Garland City, Fulton,
         Washington, Ozan, Columbus, Tollette,
         Okay, Ben Lomand, Wilton, Alleene,
         Winthrop, Ultima Thule
*Oklahoma Ghost Towns*      114
         Eagletown, Wheelock Academy, Doaksville,
         Fort Towson,  Boggy Depot, Lehigh, Clarita,
         Bromide, Fort Washita, Gene Autry,
         Dougherty, Byars, Rosedale, Tatums, Leon,
         Fleetwood, Addington, Faxon, Loveland,
         Hollister, Headrick, Elmer, Humphreys,
         Victory, Aaron School, Roosevelt,

Cooperton, Gotebo, Cloud Chief, Reed,
Vinson

*Texas Ghost Towns*                                    170

English, Jonesboro, Arthur City, Brookston,
Petty, Enloe, Ravenna, Cannon,
Westminster, Valdasta, Dorchester,
Preston, Dexter, Marysville, Myra, Bonita,
Illinois Bend, Spanish Fort, Belcherville,
Ringgold, Stoneburg, Buffalo Springs,
Shannon, Antelope, Jean, Southbend,
Eliasville, Thurber, Fort Griffin Flat,
Megargel, Mankins, Dundee, Thrift, Doan's
Crossing, Odell, Thalia, Medicine Mound,
Goodlett, Dodson, Carey, Newlin

End of the Road                                    239

Resources                                    240

"How To" plan, prepare, and research                                    248

Sources                                    253

Index                                    255

Shameless self-promotion page                                    266

## Table of Photographs

Covers: Dundee, Archer County, Texas and Aaron School, Jackson County, Oklahoma. Photos by author.

1. Thurber, TX in 1997. Photo by author.
2. Map of Red River Valley by author.
3. 1820 map of Louisiana Territory by Pierre Tardieu. David Rumsey Map collection.
4. Drawing of a Wichita village. No date, no artist. New York Public Library.
5. Red River meteorite on display at the Peabody Museum at Yale University in 2017. Photo by author.
6. Red Bird, a Comanche woman at Fort Sill, OK. No date. Library of Congress.
7. 1763 map of Louisianne, French. David Rumsey Map Collection.
8. 1820 map of Louisiana Territory by John Melish. Library of Congress.
9. 1866 map of Indian Territory. Library of Congress.
10. 1872 immigration map of Texas and Indian Territory, German. David Rumsey Map Collection.
11. 1840 sketch of Cooke's trail. Texas General Land Office (p.34).
12. 1864 print of Bailey's Dam at Alexandria from Harpers Weekly, May 1864. Library of Congress.
13. 1872 map fo Chickasaw Territory. Library of Congress.
14. 1875 Houston and Texas Central Railway map portion. Library of Congress.
15. 1937 Arkansas Highway map. Arkansas Department of Transportation.
16. Caddo, Oklahoma in 1930s by Dorothea Lange for FSA/WPA. Library of Congress.
17. Plantation store in Melrose, LA in 1940s by Mary Wolcott for FSA/WPA. Library of Congress.
18. Map of Louisiana ghost towns by Google and author.
19. Mill at Meeker, LA. Photo by author.
20. Cloutierville, LA in 1940 for HBS. Library of Congress.
21. Livingston Grocery in Cloutierville, LA in 2016. Photo by author.
22. Bank in Cloutierville, LA in 2016. Photo by author.
23. Cabins at Derry, LA in 2016. Photo by author.
24. Juke joint in Melrose, LA in 1940 by Mary Wolcott for FSA/WPA. Library of Congress.
25. Bottle garden at Oakland Plantation, Bermuda, LA. Photo by author.
26. School at Hanna, LA in 2011. Photo by author.
27. Removing the raft at Red River from papers of Lt. Woodruff, 1873. State

Library of Louisiana.
28. Hutchinson store in Caspiana, LA in 2011. Photo by author.
29. Store in Keachi, LA in 2018. Photo by author.
30. School in Keachi, LA in 2018. Photo by author.
31. Church tower in Taylortown, LA in 2011. Photo by author.
32. Calaboose in Mayers, LA in 2011. Photo by author.
33. Downtown Hosston, LA in 2015. Photo by author.
34. Satellite image of Mira, LA. By Google in 2008.
35. School in Rodessa, LA in 2015. Photo by author.
36. Map of Arkansas ghost towns by Google and author.
37. Building in Doddridge, AR. Photo by author in 2014.
38. Foundation stone in Rondo, AR. Photo by author.
39. Downtown Garland City, AR in 2014. Photo by author.
40. Bridge at Garland City, AR for HABS in 1981. Library of Congress.
41. Fulton, AR in the early 20th century. Arkansas Historical Archives.
42. 1850s map of routes to be surveyed for a transcontinental railroad. Library of Congress.
43. Downtown Fulton, AR in 2014. Photo by author.
44. Stretch of Bankhead Highway near Fulton, AR in 2014. Photo by author.
45. Tavern at Washington, AR in the 1930s. HABS. Library of Congress.
46. Franklin Street in Washington, AR in 2012. Photo by author.
47. Lodge in Washington, AR in 2018. Photo by author.
48. Lincoln School in Washington, AR in 2012. Photo by author.
49. Downtown Ozan, AR in 2018. Photo by author.
50. Former alignment of US 71, Little River County, AR in 2014. Photo by author.
51. Depot in Wilton, AR in 2014. Photo by author.
52. Calaboose in Winthrop, AR in 2014. Photo by author.
53. Map of Oklahoma ghost towns by Google and author.
54. Downtown Eagletown, OK in 2014. Photo by author.
55. Graham Grocery and post office in the 1960s in Eagletown, OK by the Daily Oklahoman, Oklahoma Historical Society.
56. 1932 hand-drawn map of Eagletown, OK by Peter Hudson in Chronicles of Oklahoma, Oklahoma Historical Society.
57. Presbyterian church at Wheelock, OK in 2009. Photo by author.
58. Post office at Doaksville, OK, not dated, by Alvin Rucker (1856-1934). Oklahoma Historical Society.

59. *Doaksville, OK structures in 1890s. B. Francis Iman Collection. Oklahoma Historical Society.*
60. *Rock base of hotel ruin in Doaksville, OK in 2002. Photo by author.*
61. *1930s hand-drawn map of Boggy Depot, OK by Muriel Wright in Chronicles of Oklahoma, Oklahoma Historical Society.*
62. *Sign in Lehigh, OK in 2015. Photo by author.*
63. *"First hotel in Bromide, OK - it belonged to Mrs. M. Johnston." Not dated. Collection of Mrs. M. Johnston. Oklahoma Historical Society.*
64. *"Farmer's Union Meeting, when Russie M. Dennis was County Organizer." Bromide, OK, 1923. Collection of Chickasaw Council House museum. Oklahoma Historical Society.*
65. *Rock Academy in the 1930s near Wapanucka, OK. Oklahoma Historical Society.*
66. *Fort Washita, OK in 2010. Photo by author.*
67. *Dougherty, OK depot in the 1960s by Daily Oklahoman, Oklahoma Historical Society.*
68. *Downtown Byars, OK. Not dated. E. R. Harrison Collection. Oklahoma Historical Society.*
69. *Downtown Rosedale, OK in 2015. Photo by author.*
70. *Tatums, OK oil refinery ad from The Black Dispatch, 1922. Oklahoma Historical Society.*
71. *Varner's Grocery and Post Office in Tatums, OK in 2015. Photo by author.*
72. *Church in Tatums, OK in 2015. Photo by author.*
73. *School in Leon, OK in 2016. Photo by author.*
74. *Vault in downtown Addington, OK in 2016. Photo by author.*
75. *Monument in Addington, OK in 2011. Photo by author.*
76. *Meridian highway near Terral, OK in 2018. Photo by author.*
77. *Building in Faxon, OK in 2017. Photo by author.*
78. *School ruin in Hollister, OK in 2017. Photo by author.*
79. *Former hotel in Headrick, OK in 2017. Photo by author.*
80. *School in Humphreys, OK in 2019. Photo by author.*
81. *Building in Victory, OK in 2019. Photo by author.*
82. *Downtown Roosevelt, OK "showing well being dug in the center of the street in front of the first bank of Roosevelt" in 1904. Peavler and Curtis Collection, Oklahoma Historical Society.*
83. *Downtown Roosevelt, OK in 2017. Photo by author.*
84. *"Opening of H. H. Wedel's big department store, March 26, 1909" in*

Gotebo, OK. Bluford E. Bryant Collection. Oklahoma Historical
Society.

85. *Downtown Gotebo, OK in 2017. Photo by author.*

86. *General store in Reed, OK in 2017. Photo by author.*

87. *Former car dealership in Vison, OK in 2017. Photo by author.*

88. *Map of Texas ghost towns by Google and author.*

89. *Boston, TX jail in 2017. Photo by author.*

90. *Arthur City, TX storm shelter in 2018. Photo by author.*

91. *Vault in Petty, TX in 2009. Photo by author.*

92. *Downtown Enloe, TX in 2017. Photo by author.*

93. *Brick building in Ravenna, TX in 2011. Photo by author.*

94. *Former school in Valdasta, TX in 2016. Photo by author.*

95. *Bank in Dorchester, TX in 2011. Photo by author.*

96. *1840 map of Texas. Library of Congress.*

97. *Preston, TX markers in 2012. Photo by author.*

98. *Vault in Dexter, TX in 2012. Photo by author.*

99. *School in Marysville, TX in 2013. Photo by author.*

100. *Ice house in Myra, TX in 2013. Photo by author.*

101. *School in Illinois Bend, TX in 2013. Photo by author.*

102. *Downtown Spanish Fort, TX in 2001. Photo by author.*

103. *1842 map of Mexico, Texas and Louisiana. David Rumsey Map Collection.*

104. *Grave of T.F. Moore at Spanish Fort, TX in 2001. Photo by author.*

105. *School in Spanish Fort, TX in 2001. Photo by author.*

106. *Downtown Ringgold, TX in 2019. Photo by author.*

107. *Gas station in Stoneburg, TX in 2013. Photo by author.*

108. *House in Buffalo Springs, TX in 2018. Photo by author.*

109. *Vault in Shannon, TX in 2018. Photo by author.*

110. *Downtown Jean, TX in 2017. Photo by author.*

111. *Mill at Eliasville, TX in 2018. Photo by author.*

112. *1960s map of Thurber in 1920. University of Texas at Arlington.*

113. *Bankhead Highway west of Ranger, TX in 2018. Photo by author.*

114. *Calaboose at Fort Griffin Flat, TX in 2017. Photo by author.*

115. *Suspension bridge in Shackleford County, TX in 2017. Photo by author*

116. *Gas station in Megargel, TX in 2016. Photo by author.*

117. *Downtown Dundee, TX in 2014. Photo by author.*

118. *Gas station in Dundee, TX in 2014. Photo by author.*

119. *Oil derricks at Thrift, TX by Homer Hardin, 1919. Library of Congress.*

120. *Topographical map of Thrift, TX, 1958. United States Geological Services, Library of Congress.*
121. *Bank at Thrift, TX in 2017. Photo by author.*
122. *Doan's Crossing adobe store in 1978. Texas Historical Commission.*
123. *Calaboose in Odell, TX in 2016. Photo by author.*
124. *Church in Thalia, TX in 2016. Photo by author.*
125. *Gas station in Medicine Mound, TX in 2016. Photo by author.*
126. *School in Medicine Mound, TX in 2016 Photo by author.*
127. *Store in Goodlett, Tx in 2014. Photo by author.*
128. *Cafe in Carey by Dorothea Lange, 1940. Farm Security Administration, Library of Congress.*
129. *Carey, TX in 2018. Photo by author.*
130. *Newlin, Tx in 2018. Photo by author.*
131. *Clarity Tunnel near Caprock Canyon State Park in 2011. Photo by author.*
132. *Palo Duro Canyon State Park in 2008. Photo by author.*

# Acknowledgements and Dedication

A good deal of gratitude is extended to Raymond Jett, my husband, who supports me one hundred percent and enjoys a good road trip; Lisa Martin Carter, my editor, whose keen understanding of language and usage astounds me; my former students who recommended some ghost towns to me; and the fantastic readers of Red River Historian, the website about "the history of where the South meets the West," who share their memories of former towns as well as their own photographs.

This book has been years in the making, as every chance I get, I find new ghost towns to explore. I love exploring them with my son David. He is a kindred spirit whose curiosity is even greater than mine. I dedicate this book to him. I love you, little buddy.

# Ghost Town Hunting in the Red River Valley

Many moons ago, I came across a little place called Thurber, Texas. My husband and I had decided on a whim to drive to Abilene, Texas from our home near Dallas, for absolutely no reason. We took Interstate 20 because my husband liked to arrive at his destinations quickly, even though we were not in a hurry.

*1.    A ruin in Thurber, Erath County, Texas.*

On our way west, I spied Thurber's long, lone chimney standing like a sentinel along the highway. I convinced my husband to stop and do some exploring. I had just graduated with my Bachelor's Degree and worked in the computer industry, and I had not become well-versed in the history of the region, yet... however, this all changed once I stepped out of the car and into Thurber. Though a thunderstorm had passed and the sky was still gray, I became deeply interested in this little place and the few remaining buildings that made up the former industrial town. I came back from this road trip convinced that one day, I would fulfill my life-long dream of becoming an historian. This, I did – all thanks to Thurber, a little town that to me, epitomizes the essence of a ghost town. (Learn about Thurber on page 206).

Today, I regularly hunt ghost towns. It has become my hobby, not unlike collecting thimbles or stamps for those with more conventional interests. Old buildings, graves, foundations, roads, and abandoned train paths link the present to the past, and hint at stories that connect to wider history. Therefore, I only capture photographs and don't pick up "keepsakes." These former communities are archeological time capsules, and I want to ensure others are able to experience and see what I do.

The ghost towns I detail in this travel guide meet two criteria: they've left behind some kind of visual reminder, and they are intertwined with their regional history. Since the Red River's confluence is over 1,300 miles long, all of the communities along the Red River's watershed and sphere of influence in northern Texas, southern Oklahoma, western

Arkansas, and northwestern/central Louisiana share stories. History isn't necessarily confined to (or defined by) an exact physical boundary. However, for the sake of road tripping, the ghost towns are grouped by state. Not every ghost town has been documented, either. The chore to make this book comprehensive in scope would be immense; therefore, some towns that may deserve the title "ghost town" may have been omitted, either by oversight or (most likely) because they will appear in a second volume about Red River Valley ghost towns.

I document my discoveries on my website, Red River Historian (www.redriverhistorian.com). My website was started to catalog the ghost towns I found, and today the site has become a collection of histories, memories, and photographs - a documentation of the history of the Red River Valley. I thoroughly enjoy my travels to "places that used to be," and with this book, I hope that readers will be able to explore these fantastic remains as well.

# **Part One**

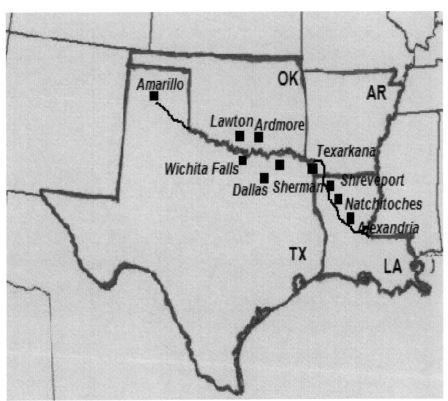

2. *The Red River Valley of the Southwest begins in Palo Duron
Canyon and runs for approximately 1,360 miles west/southwest
to the confluence of the Atchafalaya and Mississippi Rivers.
The river's truly a history of "where the South meets the West:"
it's the place where sedentary kingdoms met nomadic warriors;
where the French, Spanish, and American colonizers collided; where
the vast cattle ranches superseded the exploitative plantation
systems; and where the verdant east transitions to the unique
Cross Timbers and then gives way to the semi-arid canyons and
tablelands of the American West.*

# What Makes a Ghost Town?

Ghost towns exist all over the world. Most consist of ruins left by ancient civilizations that have become tourist attractions — think Pompeii, Machu Piccu, Angkor Wat, Troy — with the overwhelming commonality that the sites pose more questions than offer answers. Other ghost towns are of rather recent origin and have major calamities to thank for their demise, such as Pripyat at the base of the failed Chernobyl nuclear reactor, or Beichuan, China, a victim of a massive earthquake that left the city too unstable to rebuild. By contrast, American ghost towns seem rather quaint. Of much more humble and recent origins, ghost towns in the "New World" are often simply the victims of economic change. However, American ghost towns, above others, seem to capture travelers' imaginations. It's hard to gauge if it's the mythos of "manifest destiny" or the fascination with the "wild west."

But what is a ghost town, exactly? There are no hard and fast definitions. "Purists," as some ghost town hunters might be labeled, maintain that a town is officially abandoned only when it loses its post office. This explanation definitely makes sense, as towns that were recognized by the U.S. post office were able to secure funding for roads, which in turn enticed settlers and entrepreneurs. Since many towns that are seemingly abandoned still have post offices, the "post office theory" does not always offer the best definition of a ghost town.

More often than not, the railroads can be blamed for a town's demise. Many towns died when the trains bypassed them. The cities that were able to welcome tracks saw their fortunes prosper around the depots, but when the locomotives deserted them, so did their citizens. Again, there are yet many forsaken towns in which trains pass regularly (though they don't stop), so this explanation does not necessarily suffice, either.

Lastly, ghost town hunters argue that the closing of a school signals the end of a town. Schools have always been the heart and soul of American communities. This focus on literacy and democracy was the reason why the first public building erected by a community tended to be a lodge building, which could be used as a school during the week. But once the school closes and the children leave, the heart of the town declines, and the settlement slowly but surely becomes a ghost. Yet, there are several towns that have lost their schools but seem lively enough to not fall into the ghost category. For example, Robeline and Halls Summit (both in Louisiana) are still fairly active towns, even though their schools have been closed. Only time will tell if these villages will remain stable in the long run.

This leads to another quandary: what does a ghost town look like? Is it devoid of people? Does it still exist on the map? Once again, the answer is: it depends. Most ghost towns are not completely vacant, whether it's because "old timers" prefer to live in the town of their youth, retirees like the slower pace, or curmudgeons prefer the isolation. Sometimes, ghost towns exist simply as cemeteries, which serve as the only clue that a town once thrived. Yet other ghost towns are quite busy, with highways snaking their way through the community, carrying vehicles at 70 mph. Some are even located within larger cities and suburbs.

A perfect example that epitomizes this dilemma is Eagletown, Oklahoma. It began as a sparse settlement in the late 1810s by white settlers while the area was still Arkansas Territory. The town became a supply stop for Choctaws during their forced relocation in the 1830s to the newly formed Indian Territory. Soon, grists and mills, general stores, and a school served the population. Today, Eagletown still has a post office, a school, and the Union Pacific Railroad travels through, but its downtown core is abandoned, and there are no industrial or manufacturing plants. Considering its history and its current state of dilapidation, Eagletown can be considered a ghost town, though technically, it has all of the trimmings of a workable hamlet. (Learn more about Eagletown on page 113.)

Therefore, the question remains – what is a ghost town? The best answer is this: you'll know one when you see it.

# A Short History of Red River Settlement

The Red River of the South stretches across four states, each with its own unique history and people. Immense diversity defined the region since its recorded history, and several ethnic groups – Native American, African American, French, Spanish, and Anglo – put their stamps all along the river.

### Native American Settlement

Before arbitrary political divisions created modern boundaries, thousands of Native Americans called the Red River valley home. For centuries, the river formed the lifeblood for these cultures, especially in the eastern waters. Both agricultural and nomadic civilizations utilized the unique geography of the Red River to their advantage, with three tribes dominating trade and life in the years before American settlement: the Caddos, Wichitas, and Comanches.

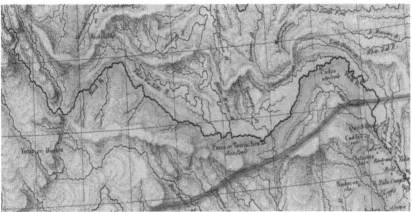

3. *1820 map of Louisiana and Red River by Pierre Tardieu (David Rumsey).*

Villages belonging to the people of common Caddoan ancestry were constructed alongside rivers to take advantage of periodic floods for natural crop irrigation. Living in today's northwestern Louisiana, southwestern Arkansas, southeastern Oklahoma, and northeastern Texas, the Caddos centered their settlements on ceremonial mounds and family compounds. The Red River figured prominently in the subsistence patterns of the Caddo Confederacy, which consisted of a number of powerful tribes with common language, custom and kinship bonds, like the Coushattas, Natchitoches, Nacogdoches, Adaes, Nasoni, and Hasinai. Hernando de Soto's 16th century expedition, for example, encountered a large Caddo village probably near today's Garland City, Arkansas or New Boston, Texas — de Soto's men were not sticklers for precise geography. Though by the time of this fateful meeting, de Soto was already dead, the new commander Luis de Moscoso and his troops burned and slashed their way through several Caddoan villages.

In the 1680s, a remnant of the La Salle expedition, guided by Henri Joutel, encountered the same tribe. Their interactions were much friendlier. The Caddos welcomed French trade, because unlike the Spanish, the French faced no restrictions on exchanging furs for guns. Both French and Spanish expeditions depicted the living conditions of the Caddos. Their villages, divided into familial compounds that included burial mounds, houses, and food storage, hugged the river.

The Caddos formed fairly good and generally peaceful relationships with the French, who built their first

permanent settlement in New France (Louisianne) in 1714 on
the Red River within the Natchitoches village. Under the
command of Louis Juchereau de St. Denis, the French built a
trading fort that was destroyed by the invading Natchez
tribe, but resurrected as a larger post and named Fort
Natchitoche, or St. Jean Baptiste. The Spanish, however,
worried that the French might dominate all trade and
alliances along the Red River. In 1729, they built a fort just a
few miles to the west of the French installation near today's
Robeline, Louisiana.

Further upstream lived the Wichitas, whose loose
amalgam of tribes spanned from central Texas into central
Kansas. Wichita tribes in the Red River Valley included the
Taovayans, Keechis, Tehucuanas, and the Tawakonis. Their
language and much of their cultural ways were kin to the
Caddoan group, but their lifestyle vacillated between
agricultural and the nomadic hunting cultures of the Plains
tribes.

The first sustained contact with colonial powers in the
Red River Valley amongst the Wichita tribes centered on
Bernard de la Harpe in the 1720s, after St. Denis had tasked
him to establish trading posts along the Red River north of
Natchitoches. De la Harpe placed a post within the Nasoni
(Caddoan) village along the Great Bend of the Red River,
then appeared to have made contact with the a substantial
Taovayan village that spanned the Red River between
today's Jefferson County, Oklahoma and Montague County,
Texas. Athanase de Mezieres, a Frenchman who became an
envoy for Spain when the Spanish took control of the
Louisiana Territory in 1763, named the village San Bernardo

(on the north side) and San Teodoro (on the south side). Though some historical accounts believed the villages to be French in origin, archeological digs concluded that the substantial settlement was present before European contact.

In 1759, the Taovayans and the Comanches raided the San Saba mission (near today's Menard, Texas) about 200 miles to the south of their villages. This may have been because the mission supported the Apaches, sworn enemies of the Comanches. The attack killed several monks and soldiers, led to the theft of several horses, and left the mission in ruins. The Governor of New Spain sent Diego Ortiz Parilla and six hundred men to pursue the Indians. The Spanish troops followed their trail to the Taovayan villages and attacked, but realized quickly that they were on the losing end. Over one thousand warriors lived at San Bernardo and San Teodoro, and they easily repelled the Spanish forces. A few decades later, both disease and tribal warfare diminished the Tayovayans, who then abandoned the village. When American settlers found evidence of this short but intense battle, they mistakenly named the town they built there "Spanish Fort." (See page 193).

4.A Wichita village (NYPL).

The Wichitas truly mirrored the geography of the central Red River valley. They lived in the Cross Timbers, a dominant landscape feature which consisted of long, dense, and narrow strands of post and blackjack oaks, hackberries, pecans, cottonwoods, and elms interspersed by the Grand Prairie. These "cast iron forests," as writer Washington Irving described them when he visited Texas in the 1830s, marked the transition from a well-watered, agricultural region to arid grasslands in which subsistence relied on seasonal hunts. The Wichita tribes lived like this as well: they cultivated corn, squash, beans, sunflowers, pumpkins, and melons, but also hunted bison.

Bison hunting brought the Wichitas into the world of the Comanches, with whom they shared both trading and spiritual relationships. On the prairies south of the villages lay several meteorites, including one of the largest specimens in North America, which weighed over 1,600 pounds. To the Panis — which is how early American traders called the Wichitas — these extraterrestrial boulders provided medicine. The Comanches named the meteorites, a practice that mirrored their veneration of the rocks. In 1808, an American filibustering party led by Henry Glass took the largest meteorite, which the Comanche had named Po-a-cat-le-pi-le-carre, in an expedition most likely financed by Dr. John Sibley, the Indian Agent stationed in Natchitoches. While the Americans called this "a retrieval," the action was actually outright theft, as the tribes and New Spain both claimed the land it sat on. The Americans believed the rock to be a platinum treasure, which of course it wasn't; instead of wealth, the iron mass held only scientific value to the

Americans. It eventually ended up inside the Peabody Collection of Yale University. The effect of the theft of the medicine stone on the tribes may have been immeasurable. Immediately after its theft, Wichita history entered a "dark period" of warfare, disease, and hunger. At the same time, the Comanches amped up their war against American incursions.

*5.The Red River Meteorite is now housed in the Peabody Museum at Yale University.*

Access to the horse allowed the Comanches to dominate the Red River Valley, specifically in the west. Thanks to this new technology, Comanche influence and power grew at the same time the Spanish established their empire in the New World. Thus, when the Spanish were ready to penetrate into the lands north of San Antonio, they encountered a formidable empire that claimed a vast territory known as the Comancheria.

Several bands formed the tribe collectively known as the Comanches. Men and women followed leaders who convinced them of their visions. Most of the bands devoted themselves to warfare. Comanche men divided their time between hunting bison and raiding foes. They set up semi-permanent camps along creeks that fed into the Red and Brazos rivers, following bison herds as well as enemy tribes. While violence towards other Indians like the Tonkawas was common, the Comanches also established trading relationships, especially with the Comancheros (people of Comanche and Spanish descent). Comanches and Comancheros traded vessels, cloth fabric, buffalo hides, guns, and even ransomed captives. These captives often came from raids that the Comanches staged against Mexican and American settlements. While children caught up in the raids were often adopted into the tribe, the Indians either killed or enslaved the adults. Survivors could be ransomed by their families or the state, using trusted Comanchero traders as intermediaries. Much of this illicit trade was carried out along the Texas caprock.

6.*Red Bird, a Comanche woman at Fort Sill, Oklahoma (LOC).*

The caprock is a long, north-south geological fissure that indicates a sudden rise in elevation as the Cross Timbers gives way to the Staked Plains. It extends all the way to Palo Duro Canyon, the birthplace of the Red River and the site of the final battles of the Red River Wars in the mid-1870s. The wars marked the defeat of the southern Plains tribes, who were forced to settle on the reservation at Fort Sill, many as subsistence farmers.

### French and Spanish Settlement

The first permanent "Old World" settlers to make the Red River their home were the French, who founded plantations along the river to the south of the Natchitoches village (a Caddoan tribe) in Louisiana in the early eighteenth century. Along with slaves brought from the Caribbean, French settlers established large operations in the hopes of growing tobacco to compete against English tobacco farms in Virginia. Each plantation had private docks that jutted into tributaries of the Red River, such as Bayou Boeuf, or the Red River itself. From these docks, the planters sent flat boats filled with cash crops down river to markets in either Natchez, Mississippi or New Orleans.

7.A 1763 French map of French Louisiana shows that the Red River constituted the furthest west of the territory's reaches (David Rumsey).

The operations proved very profitable, allowing the enslaved population to grow. Many "new" families were born from relationships between French men and African/Caribbean women. Over the years, they self-identified as Creole (from the Latin word, "created") to differentiate themselves from the Anglos (English-speakers). One prominent family in particular began with the liaison between Marie Therese Coincoin and Louis Pierre Metoyer, who freed her and their children. Coincoin established her own plantation on a Spanish land grant. Her family erected the first church founded by freedmen in the Red River Valley, St. Augustine, in 1823. Many of the Creole settlements are now ghost towns, all preserved in the Cane River Creole National Heritage Area south of today's Natchitoches (see page 64).

Between 1763 and 1800, French Louisiana came under the dominion of New Spain. The Spanish did not change the customs of native tribes nor the Creoles. They did, however, bring structure to the eastern Red River. For example, the Spanish preferred building with brick and iron, making for more permanent architecture. This is evidenced in New Orleans, where most of the Old Quarter contains not French, but Spanish structures. They introduced sugar cane cultivation to the southern Red River Valley, which instigated a more intense slave trade. And, to ensure essential troop movement and continuous communication, the New Spanish government extended the Camino de Real (Royal Road) into Natchitoches, thus connecting the Red River to San Antonio. Further, Spain had granted Americans navigation rights to the Mississippi River and its tributaries under the Treaty de San Lorenzo in 1795. The heightened economic activity led to the establishment of more land grants. Today's Alexandria and Marksville, Louisiana, to name two prominent river towns, began as centers of Spanish land grants.

In 1800, France regained the Louisiana Territory from Spain in the secret Treaty of San Ildefonso. Though this new development alarmed the Americans once they found out about it, the French could not afford this renewed land wealth, mainly because of the revolution storming through Haiti. In 1803, Napoleon offered the entire territory to the United States for $15 million. Although the Louisiana Purchase faced stiff opposition from some members of Congress, native Louisianans, and created a constitutional crisis, the U.S. bought the territory. Without a survey, the Red River Valley ended up constituting an international border, or a "no man's land."

### *American Settlement*

American culture is based on reason, so in typical American fashion, the U.S. set out set out to explore, document, map, and catalog its newly acquired territory. In addition to ordering the famous Missouri River Expedition of 1804, President Thomas Jefferson outfitted a party to traverse the Red River from Natchitoches in 1806. Helmed by Peter Custis, Thomas Freeman, and Richard Sparks, this Corps of Discovery was tasked with surveying the southern boundary of the Louisiana Territory. Because Jefferson knew that the Red River had been used as a conduit to Santa Fe by Spanish and French traders, he also hoped that the river would prove navigable enough to allow river traffic into New Spain, thus opening up more trading opportunities.

In May of 1806, the Custis, Freeman and Sparks
expedition set out to explore the Red River. They
immediately got bogged down by the Great Raft, however.
For centuries, the area north and northeast of Natchitoches
consisted of a vast series of swamps and lakes, created by a
massive log jam that accumulated just north of the Grand
Ecore, a distinctive bluff that marked a change in the river's
depth levels.

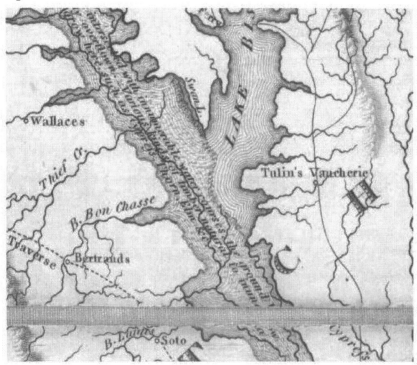

8.*John Melish's map from 1820 explains the Great Raft of
the Red River: "Intersected with innumerable water courses the
ground... overflown. Various kinds of timber natural to
inundation grown here, such as Cypress, Thorn, Elm, etc" (LOC).*

The jam backed up the river for hundreds of miles,
generating floods that assisted the Caddos in irrigating their

fields but also impeding river-going traffic and discouraging European settlement. It took the Corps almost a month to find their way out of the bogs and onto the main channel of the river, and then only with the help of two Caddoan guides, Cut Finger and Grand Ozages. Ultimately, the expedition was cut short when Spanish commander Francisco Viana intercepted their voyage at Spanish Bluff on the southern bank of the river in today's Bowie County, claiming that the Americans were trespassing on Spanish land. Since the Americans were not attempting to start a war with New Spain, they acquiesced and abandoned their journey. Luckily, Custis and Freeman published their discoveries, which included the first map of the Red River above Natchitoches.

Americans began moving into the Red River Valley by the early 1810s. By 1816, Louisiana was admitted to the union, and the rest of the Louisiana Purchase became known as Missouri Territory. In 1819, Arkansas Territory separated from Missouri Territory. Arkansas Territory consisted of a large swath of land that stretched from the Mississippi River in the east to the thirty-sixth parallel in the north and encompassed today's Oklahoma to the one-hundredth meridian. The territory became a sticking point for the Missouri Compromise of 1820 — it was the area that Congress allowed Missouri to "choose" if it wanted to enter the union as a free or slave state.

The Americans settled all around the eastern Red River in both Louisiana and Arkansas. Many founded plantations, heavily based on slavery by African Americans who came from as far away as Virginia to be sold "down river" in the horrific Three Forks market in Natchez, Mississippi. Others sought bison, otter, and beaver furs. Some ventured as far west as southeastern Oklahoma and as far south as northeastern Texas. Depending on their politics and which nation protected them against Indians, free Americans in northeastern Texas either claimed to be citizens of New Spain (by 1821, Mexican Texas) or of Miller County, Arkansas Territory.

The confusion stemmed from an 1812 survey of the international boundary between the United States and Mexico conducted by William Darby. John Melish's map of the Louisiana Territory in 1816 and the Adams-Onis Treaty of 1819 both relied on the faulty survey. To bring order into this "no-mans land," the U.S. Congress charged Major J.D. Graham and Lt. Col. Kearney with measuring a new survey, which they successfully did in 1840 near Logansport, Louisiana. By then, the international boundary stood between the United States and the Republic of Texas.

Several new American market towns developed in the Red River valley prior the Civil War. Fulton, La Grange, Lost Prairie, Rondo, Blevins, and Washington were settled in Arkansas Territory and in Mexican Texas, Americans filibustered into settlements like Jonesboro, Boston, English, and Pecan Point. When the Spanish gave Moses Austin the first legal land grant in southern Texas in 1821, some of the "Original 300" settlers crossed the Red River at Fulton, Arkansas Territory, where Stephen F. Austin, Moses's son, set up a trading post in anticipation of their arrival.

### Slavery in the Red River Valley

Anglo Americans who came to the Red River Valley brought with them the southern-style slave system. Here, they established new plantations that produced cotton, tobacco, sugar cane, pecans, and corn. Cattle drovers and stockmen also owned slaves. The border disputes and isolation of the Red River Valley led to a number of escapes amid the brutal living conditions. Several enslaved people escaped into Mexican Texas after Mexico outlawed slavery in 1824, and after 1850, Americans of Mexican descent even formed an underground railroad to safely guide escaping people into Mexico. This did not stop the importation of more slaves in the ensuing decades before the Civil War, however. The numbers of enslaved people continued to increase, although the numbers of slave owners remained relatively small (for example, less than thirty percent of Texans owned ninety percent of other human beings). No major slave markets existed in the Red River Valley — slave auctions and speculations were mainly confined to either Natchez or New Orleans. After 1836, people freed from slavery through probates in Arkansas were not allowed to stay in the state; they either had to relocate or voluntarily re-enslave themselves. Every legislative session in the Republic of Texas (1836-1845) and after statehood from 1845 to 1865 dealt with pleas by freed people to remain in the state. They had to find witnesses to attest to their "good character" to keep their homes.

In Indian Territory, a new slave society appeared along the Red River Valley by the 1820s and 1830s. The Choctaws, whose original homelands comprised the

Mississippi River region between Louisiana and Mississippi, arrived in Indian Territory as the first signatories of a Mississippi state removal treaty. The tribe introduced the southern slave system, as some of the more prominent part-European members had adopted American Southern economies and customs. By the 1840s, when the Chickasaws settled in Indian Territory, slavery had become a firmly established institution all along the Red River, from its source to its mouth.

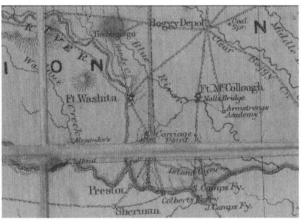

9.*For a few decades, all roads in Indian Territory led to Boggy Depot (LOC).*

### *Indian Nations*

In 1828, the United States established Indian Territory out of Arkansas Territory to accommodate southeastern Indian tribes who were forcibly removed from their homelands due to treaties that the federal government enforced through the Indian Removal Act of 1830. Several towns in the Red River Valley received some federal monies to accommodate the migrants, such as Paraclifta and Washington, Arkansas, and some towns, like Ultima Thule, Arkansas, were founded specifically to supply the migrants.

While the Choctaws and Chickasaws entered Indian Territory at Eagletown, most settled further west near the newly erected Fort Towson. The fort, established in 1824, served to protect the migrant tribes from Anglo, Osage, and Comanche hostilities. Near the fort, the Choctaws founded Doaksville (see page 121). The tribe also opened schools within their new territory to ensure that their children would not be sent to far-away boarding schools to become "Americanized." With the assistance of Presbyterian missionaries and important education advocates like the Choctaw Reverend Israel Folsom, the Choctaws established Wheelock Academy in 1832, Spencer Academy in 1842, and Armstrong Academy in 1845. Towards the western part of the Choctaw lands, the Chickasaws founded Boggy Depot to center their nation. They opened their own schools, such as Bloomfield Academy in 1852, Wapanucka Academy in 1852, and Burney Academy in 1859. By the 1930s, the academies shut their doors in favor of an integrated approach to education, and most of the buildings fell to ruins.

The Caddos, the once-prominent tribe of the eastern Red River, lost their homelands through a series of treaties and land sales as Anglos and the migrant tribes squeezed them out. They found a new home (albeit temporary) around Caddo Lake, an inlet formed from the Great Raft that straddled the border between Texas and Louisiana. By the 1850s, Texans forced the Caddos to move to the Brazos Indian Reservation in the arid Cross Timbers region of north central Texas. Hostility from the whites and other tribes within the reservation necessitated their final move to the

Wichita Agency in the area around Anadarko in Indian Territory. The Caddos now share lands with the Wichitas.

### Transportation in the Red River Valley

The Great Raft proved a major obstacle to river boat traffic along the Red River. Early plans called for digging canals around the raft, but Arkansas and Louisiana governors wanted the channel cleared. Thus, the federal government tasked the Army Corps of Engineers to remove the log jam and hired Henry Shreve to manage the project in 1832. Shreve was well-known for his previous river clearings, and came to the Red River prepared with a new contraption — the Heliopolis, a snag boat that removed logs and cut them into chips at the same time. The project cost $25,000 and took five years, but its success led to the founding of Shreveport, Louisiana in 1836. It also created new opportunities at Caddo Lake, which was now opened to unimpeded navigation. With the river cleared, the Big Cypress Creek, a branch of the Red River, allowed Jefferson, Texas, established in 1842, to become a deep-water port. Both Shreveport and Jefferson flourished as bustling market centers. Natchitoches did not fare so well, however. With the raft's removal, the fabled French city found itself removed from the main river channel. By the turn of the twentieth century, Cane River, which was the oxbow lake that formed at Natchitoches after the raft's removals, was dammed to permanently seal the river from the main channel.

Meanwhile, Captain Henry Shreve warned that without sustained maintenance, the river would jam once again. The federal government did not provide any new funds to keep the river open, and slowly but surely, the raft returned. In 1873, the Army Corps of Engineers dynamited the log jam. This act drained the Big Cypress Bayou in Texas, leaving Jefferson dry-docked. Without access to the river, the city dwindled in importance.

*10. Opening up the Great Raft led to the middle Red River becoming a destination for migrants. This 1872 German map points to a number of settlements made possible by improved transportation (David Rumsey).*

The clearing of the raft allowed for increased river boat traffic, and several towns appeared along the Red River touting themselves as the "heads of navigation" – Laynesport, Arkansas, and Jonesboro, Texas, for example. These river towns do not exist anymore.

Transportation was not simply confined to river traffic, however. The unpredictability of fluctuating water levels made road building an important early task, and more often than not, the military carved roads beyond the established settlements in Arkansas and Louisiana. Military roads led to Fort Towson in Indian Territory and also linked various post offices. National roads were proposed but weren't completed. By the 1850s, stage coach lines from northeastern Texas transported travelers to Washington, Arkansas and Shreveport. Many of the stagecoach routes have become state highways, but some of the stagecoach towns, like Cannon, Texas have succumbed to neglect (see page 181).

Other roads served as emigrant trails for people bound for Texas. Several trails crossed the Red River: Trammel Trace from Arkansas Territory and Indian Territory into Texas, Camino de Real from Louisiana into Texas, and the aptly named Texas Trail in Indian Territory. Texas Trail ran from Missouri to Colbert's Ferry at the Red River. Once in Texas, the road, often referenced as Preston Trail, journeyed south through Dallas to Waco and ultimately, to San Antonio. By the early 1850s, this road saw the first north-bound cattle drives out of Texas — this portion of the trail has been called Shawnee Trail. In the late 1850s, portions of Texas Trail served the Butterfield Overland Mail and Stagecoach line, the first transcontinental stagecoach in the Southwest.

Several ferry operations appeared along the Red River to accommodate the increasing mobility. The ferries were often connected to privately-owned trading forts, such as Warren and Preston in Texas. Other ferry crossings became little hamlets in their own right due to the accommodations they offered, such as Colbert in Indian Territory, Garland City in Arkansas and Fulton in Arkansas (see pages 92 and 95).

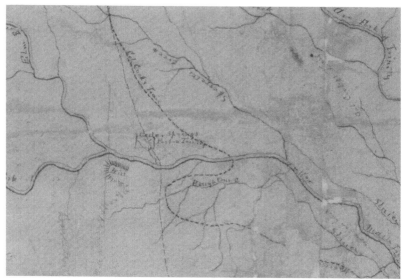

11.*Early trails begat major places – Cedar Springs along Cooke's Trail (Preston Road) in northern Texas is now more widely known as Dallas (1840, TX GLO).*

## *Mapping the Red River Valley*

The western portion of the Red River — beyond the ninety-eighth meridian — remained largely unmapped by the United States and only sparsely settled by Americans during the first half of the nineteenth century. This would gradually change after Randolph B. Marcy and George B. McClellan were charged with surveying the western Red River in 1852. Marcy was infinitely qualified to make this journey. As a captain in the Army Corps of Engineers, he had surveyed a proposed route for a transcontinental railroad that would cross Arkansas and Texas; mapped the headwaters of several rivers and creeks within Texas for German emigrant companies; and had established Fort Arbuckle in Indian Territory in 1850. He also wrote a how-to guide for traveling through the hostile prairies.

Embarking from Preston, Texas (see page 185), a town that grew up around Holland Coffee's trading post, Marcy's expedition followed the old Spanish Road that paralleled the northern side of the Red River. After a three-month journey, during which Marcy cataloged the geology, flora and fauna found around the western portion of the river, Marcy completed his mission when he discovered the headwaters of both the Salt Fork and Prairie Dog Town Fork of the Red River. He and his men returned to a hero's welcome, once the soldiers at Fort Arbuckle recovered from their surprise that he and his party were still alive – rumors had spread that the expedition had met a gruesome fate at the hands of the Comanches.

### The Red River and the Civil War

By 1860, the eastern flow of the Red River — from the Chickasaw Nation, Indian Territory/Grayson County, Texas eastward to the river's confluence into the Mississippi River in Louisiana — had become a lively affair, with market towns, steamboat travel, well-graded roads, prosperous farms, and large plantations. A few railroads had been proposed but none actually built (save for a portion of the Texas and Pacific Railway between Shreveport and Marshall). However, the Civil War brought a brief end to advancement, as most counties, Indian nations, and parishes either shifted their resources, or lost them, in the ensuing fight.

Loyalties were very much divided during the conflict. After the Kansas conflicts in the late 1850s, fear of slave insurrections and infiltration of abolitionists induced mob killings throughout the Red River Valley. Additionally, many free, white men who lived in the Red River Valley were either Whigs or Union Democrats — they preferred free-soil rather than slavery expansion — and voted against secession. Retaliation by slaver Democrats was often swift and brutal, and the 1862 Confederate draft in particular stirred up latent hostilities. In Gainesville, Texas forty men, accused of treason because they opposed the conditions of the draft, were hanged in two mass lynchings. This violence beckoned outlaws like William Quantrill and his gang (which included Jesse James and Cole Younger) into the Red River Valley, where their presence stirred up lots of unease.

The general lawlessness during the Civil War afflicted Indian Territory particularly hard. The Choctaw and Chickasaw Nations were not immune to the violence. The members of the nations who were largely of European descent condoned the slave economy and joined forces with Texas Confederates. They roamed the area, ransacking farms and participating in battles around Fort Washita, Boggy Depot, Honey Springs, and Camden. The outlaw gangs and political divisions terrorized the citizens in Indian Territory. Many fled into Kansas, leaving farms and livestock behind. Formerly prosperous families became destitute after the Civil War.

The Red River figured prominently in the war after Union forces took control of both Arkansas and Louisiana in 1863. Though the Union troops occupied the capitals of both states, rebels still held the western portions, and Texas lay beyond that. The Union army staged three campaigns to enter Texas via the Red River. Their Indian Territory campaign was quickly repelled, as was the Union's Camden

Campaign in Arkansas. In Louisiana, General Porter took boats up the Red River to lend support to General Nathaniel Banks planned invasion of Texas, but after losing to the Confederates at Mansfield, the gun boats bogged down by low water in the rapids at Alexandria. Union engineer Bailey designed a series of simple dams to float the boats over the rapids.

12.*Harper's Weekly depicted the damming over the rapids at Alexandria in their May 1864 issue (LOC).*

In Texas, the Civil War played out differently. Though Texas seceded from the Union like the rest of the Confederacy because it wanted to preserve slavery, the state also reprimanded the federal government for not protecting its citizens from Indian attacks. Forts like Belknap, Cooper, and Worth had been established in the antebellum period along what the military called the "frontier line," but the military outposts did not do much to curtail depredations by Comanches during the war. After the war, the U.S. carved reservations for the Indians in Indian Territory, all the while establishing more army forts as it prepared for the final wars with the Plains Indians. Forts Sill, Supply, Richardson, and

Griffin were erected to commandeer troops, and settlements, like Fort Griffin Flat (see page 214), appeared around them to support and supply them.

### Reconstruction along the Red River

The reconstruction period (1865- 1877) brought progress but also a lot of uncertainty to citizens — which now included freed slaves — who lived along the river. African Americans may have gained freedom and black men may have gained suffrage, but they encountered much racial violence. Secret dens of the Ku Klux Klan appeared in almost all counties and parishes. The Freedmen's Bureau, established by congress to protect voting rights and ensure that African American laborers were not mistreated or re-enslaved, recorded many incidents of terror, which lasted for almost a century. In the 1870s, a white mob in Colfax, Louisiana killed 150 black militia members in an attempt to reestablish "white supremacy," a term commemorated on a marker in the town's cemetery. In 1893, one of the most horrific "spectacle lynchings" took place in Paris, Texas. A crowd of over 10,000 people watched as a man was tortured to death. In the 1910s, the entire black population of Whitesboro, Texas was pushed to leave town. Lynchings, whippings, and adverse possession of property owned by blacks took place in almost every single county along the Red River.

Civil rights leaders and newspaper editors encouraged African Americans to move away from the racism in their home areas and settle in Indian Territory, where they hoped to establish new, insular communities away from white racism. New treaties forced on the nations in Indian Territory after the Civil War made this resettlement possible, and so several freedmen towns emerged: Tatums (see page 138), Lima, and Homer, to name a few.

Schools became a very important component of reconstruction. Prior to the Civil War, high schools in Louisiana, Texas, and Arkansas were based on subscription — meaning that in order to attend, one had to pay tuition. Poor whites who couldn't afford these private schools were thus barred from education, and enslaved people were legally not allowed to learn reading and writing at all. While this system definitely helped the planter society in supplying a steady form of manual labor, it had an overall detrimental effect on social and economic progress. In order for the states to be readmitted into the Union, Congressional reconstruction demanded that they make access to education a state constitutional right, supported by land grants and public funds. Schools were built in hundreds of communities, and these communities grew into towns. Schools were segregated by race, both physically and financially. Desegregation in the latter part of the twentieth century, coupled with population shifts from rural to urban centers, closed many of the smaller schools, which resulted in a number of ghost towns. Good examples of this can be found all over the Red River Valley, from Gotebo, Oklahoma (see page 164) to St. Matthew, Louisiana (see page 65).

New industries began building in earnest during reconstruction, too. Business took advantage of the region's ties to its agricultural past on an industrial scale: namely, cotton and cattle. Cotton quickly regained its title as the Southwest's staple crop, with towns like Shreveport and Dallas becoming major cotton hauling and processing centers. Cottonseed oil mills and textile mills appeared all over the region. The longhorn, a cattle breed that ran feral throughout southern Texas and northern Mexico, had been trailed before the Civil War into Louisiana and Missouri; after the war, Joseph McCoy, a livestock dealer from Illinois,

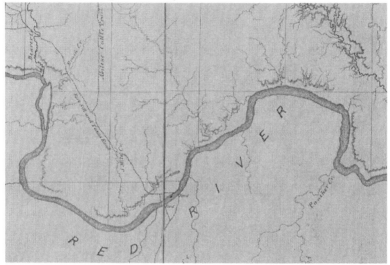

13.The Abilene cattle trail extended from Kansas to Indian Territory. Texans crossed at Red River Station in today's Montague County (1872, LOC).

promoted parts of an established trace through Indian Territory and called it the Abilene Trail (this would become known by its more famous name, the Chisholm Trail). Millions of cattle would be ferried from Texas to the railhead in Abilene, Kansas along this route. Many were sold along the way to Choctaw, Chickasaw, and Cherokee ranchers, or to the Indian reservations in the western part of the territory. Most of the cattle, though, ended up in the massive slaughterhouses of Kansas City, Chicago, and St. Louis. As farms, ranches, and settlements continued to encroach westward, the Western Trail, which reached from Texas into the Dakotas, supplanted the trail. The encroachment of farms on the open lands led to "range wars," as drovers believed it was their right to trail cattle. The barbed wire fence, increased rail transportation, and refrigeration put an end to the cattle trails.

### Red River Rails

Beginning in the 1870s, thousands of miles of tracks were laid across the region. The Missouri-Kansas-Texas Railroad (MKT) won a federal contest to receive the first right-of-way through Indian Territory and built its line parallel to the Texas Road. Entering Indian Territory in 1871, the MKT reached across the Red River in 1872, founding Denison, Texas as its southern terminus. The St. Louis, Iron Mountain and Southern Railway laid its route into Fulton, Arkansas in 1874, then extended its tracks into the new city of Texarkana, which was platted by the Texas and Pacific Railway (T&P). The T&P then began building westward into Dallas, where in 1872 it crossed paths with the Houston and Texas Central Railway (H&TC). Louisiana's rail network between the Mississippi and Red rivers was well established before the Civil War, especially in Alexandria. The T&P Railroad, Illinois Central Railroad, and others crossed the state after the war.

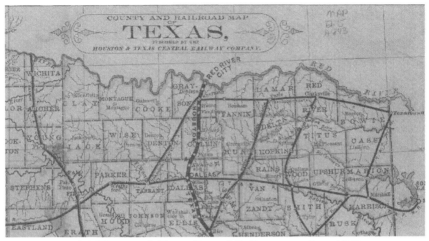

14.A Houston & Texas Central Railway map from 1875
also shows other railroad networks in north Texas (LOC).

Soon, new towns, many built on speculation by the
railroad corporations, sprung up along the tracks all over the
southwest, beckoning to people with jobs and commerce.
This boom had a down-side, however. Antebellum towns
that were ideally situated before the railroads came through
suddenly found themselves bypassed. Washington,
Arkansas (see page 99) saw traffic shift to Hope, which was
founded as a land speculation deal by the Texas and Pacific
Railway. Dexter, Texas (see page 188) gradually gave way to
Gainesville. The railroad corporations can be thanked (or
cursed, depending on your vantage point) for many ghost
towns that inhabit the Red River Valley.

The railroads brought new homesteaders, of course.
The tracks opened the "frontier" to people who wanted to
make their homes on the prairie, especially in Indian
Territory. To release this land to American settlers, the
federal government first had to bar the Native Americans
from using it. The initial step was the reservation system,

originating at the Medicine Lodge Creek Treaty for the Southern Plains Indians in 1864. The Kiowas, Comanches, and others did not necessarily abide by this treaty, of course — reservation lands were militarized and hard-scrabble. Many continued to live in their traditional ways. The Red River Wars of 1875 changed that, as the defeat of the tribes placed the last holdouts of the southern Plains tribes onto reservations in western Indian Territory. Then, the Indian nations were forced by the Dawes Act of 1887 to privatize their land holdings with individual allotments. The lands that had been theirs for decades were re-distributed through a series of land lotteries. The first such give-a-way occurred in 1889, but many others followed. Soon, the western half of Indian Territory became Oklahoma Territory and new towns emerged, like Mangum and Hollis. Though the Kiowas protested these land grabs, the Supreme Court sided with the United States, and the privatization of tribal lands continued.

### *Red River Roads*

Transportation continued to redefine the Red River Valley throughout the twentieth century. While railroads busily constructed right-of-ways, roads began to multiply, too. At first, the gradual shift from railroads to highways was barely noticeable. Bicyclists championed "good roads" in order to have smooth pavement on which to ride their safety bicycles. Their clubs spawned a progressive-era movement that sought federal and state funding for road projects. Automobile enthusiasts expanded these erst-while private "good roads" into a series of traveling paths on which to enjoy the loud and noxious "horseless carriage." The Bankhead Highway, Jefferson Highway, Dixie Overland Highway, Meridian Highway, Hobby Highway, Robert E. Lee Highway, King of Trails Highway, and Ozark Trail soon stretched across the Red River landscape.

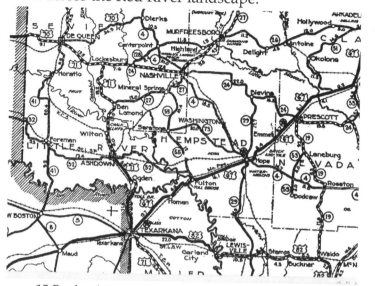

15.Roads crisscrossed the Great Bend in 1937 (AR DoT).

After World War I, General Jack Pershing recommended lacing the United States with a series of well-maintained roads in order to move military equipment efficiently, and the government heeded the recommendation. In 1926, federal highway acts replaced the names of private highways with a system of numbers, and federal money began pouring into the states to build and maintain thoroughfares. Towns and cities thrived on the increased traffic, and competed for tourist money. In Arkansas, the Ozarks and Hot Springs beckoned. In Oklahoma, spa cities like Sulphur, Bromide (see page 131), and Medicine Park enticed visitors. In Texas, one could find relaxation along the Bankhead Highway at Mineral Wells.

All of this economic activity meant one thing – Americans needed oil, and lots of it. In the early part of the twentieth century, the Red River Valley saw its fair share of oil boom towns. Northwestern Louisiana became home to Rodessa (see page 84), Oil City and Vivian. In northwestern Texas and southwestern Oklahoma, tent cities appeared around oil wells and then quickly succumbed when either the fields dried out or investors mismanaged funds, like Thrift west of Burkburnett, Texas (see page 221). All four states that claim the Red River feature boom and bust oil cities, a phenomenon that continues to the present day.

### *Red River Dust*

The Great Depression of the 1930s devastated the Red River Valley. Sharecropping, a dominant activity along the eastern portions of the Red River, failed miserably as mechanization and scientific management took over. Thousands of farmers were displaced and sought refuge in larger cities, leaving many old plantations to succumb to the bulldozer. Towards the west, the situation was just as dire. Large farms, many tenant- occupied or mortgaged, had prospered during World War I as the United States became the largest exporter of wheat to the rest of the world. The farming methods that produced this abundance, however, left the soil in poor condition and over-exposed. Without the aboriginal prairie grasses to anchor the soil, the high winds and drought conditions in the staked plains of Texas and Oklahoma lifted the dirt from the ground. This became the largest man-made disaster the United States had ever witnessed: the Dust Bowl. Like sharecroppers from the

*16.In the late 1930s, Dorothea Lange photographed the effects of the Great Depression in Caddo, Bryan County, Oklahoma (LOC).*

South, farmers in the West abandoned their homes in order to find work elsewhere. Many of the Dust Bowl refugees found work in California, particularly in the Central Valley surrounding Bakersfield. The forced migration of "Okies" (a disparaging moniker created by Californians to describe farmers fleeing the Dust Bowl) constituted one of the largest Diasporas in the United States. Whole communities were abandoned during these hard times; to this day, much of the lands in the plains and on the prairie still have not recovered from this environmental calamity.

The central portion of Texas' Red River Valley fared much better, mainly because of its political champion, Sam Rayburn. Rayburn, who grew up in Fannin County, Texas, served in the Texas and U.S. House of Representatives from

1907 to 1961. During the last twenty years he was Speaker of the House (U.S.) except for a short interval. A progressive Democrat and supporter of Roosevelt's New Deal, Rayburn brought lots of federal money into northern Texas, including financing Lake Texoma, construction of which began in 1939. The damming of the Red River at the Washita River meant that many settlements west of Denison, Texas and Colbert, Oklahoma would be deluged, and the towns of Willis, Oklahoma and Cedar Mill, Texas were drowned.

### The Modern Red River Valley

World War II brought prosperity back to the whole region as the Red River Valley had important allies in Washington D.C. Dallas, Fort Worth, Wichita Falls, Shreveport, Alexandria, Texarkana, and Lawton became hubs for military and industrial activity. Towns that had been simple farming centers surrounding these larger towns began to grow, with new neighborhoods built to accommodate the many factory workers hired to support the war effort. The populations of smaller towns shrunk as cities continued to beckon in the post-war period, allowing suburbs like Oak Cliff, Texas, Bossier City, Louisiana, and Plano, Texas to sprawl. Connecting these manufacturing centers to the affordable housing in the outlying towns required new roads to handle the increased traffic, and the Interstate Highway system, built in the Eisenhower era as a public works program, helped to develop new towns.

Americans, including those who lived in the Red River Valley, had fallen in love with the automobile. Sleek and fast highways, such as Interstates 35, 30, and 20, coupled with increased air travel, rapidly replaced the old highway and railroad systems. The streetcars and interurbans quickly gave way to car and bus travel. By the 1970s, passenger rail in the Red River Valley had effectively ceased. This caused the gradual decline of several towns that had their fortunes tied to the railroads, like Dougherty, Oklahoma (see page 135). The efficiency of the Interstate Highways also led to the demise of small villages, like Myra, Texas (see page 190), as bypasses and franchises along the Interstates siphoned business from downtown cores.

Today, the Red River Valley is in the midst of another massive transformation — the growth of urban centers with their burgeoning technological infrastructure, and the decline of rural living. Much of the changes have yet to fully play out, but the handwriting is on the wall, so to speak. Towns sitting on the old highways are slowly seeing their inhabitants leave for opportunities that only the cities can afford them. The right-of-ways of rail lines that once saw daily passenger service have been abandoned, and the towns that thrived alongside the tracks seem to be in a state of suspended shock as their lifeblood drains away.

The Red River Valley is littered with the remains of towns that progress bypassed. Let's explore them.

# Part Two

*17.Melrose, Natchitoches Parish, Louisiana in the 1940s. This photograph was taken by Mary Wolcott for the Farm Security Administration (LOC).*

## *Ghost Towns in the Red River Valley*

When it comes to history, it becomes very difficult to ascertain which came first — which tribe staked their claim on the land first, which European nation asserted their authority first, which American settler built the first farm… and on it goes. The "firsts" depends on perspectives and geographic vantage points. To make the ghost town hunt easier, the historical timeline will be marked by the Louisiana Purchase of 1803, when the Red River began its journey to become part of the United States. Thus, Louisiana (founded in 1812) is the first state we visit. Then, we'll jog into Arkansas, which was carved out of Missouri Territory in 1819 and entered the Union in 1836. Next, we'll discover Indian Territory (today's Oklahoma), which began its official life in 1824 after its split with Arkansas Territory and received statehood in 1907. Lastly, we'll explore Texas, which entered the union in 1845.

Texas is a good state to end this journey because its panhandle is the birthplace of the Red River. Is it strange that we end at the head and begin at the mouth? Not really. In the Red River Valley, the history of human settlement progresses upriver, for both Native American and European migration. The further north and west the Red River flows, the younger the settlements tend to be. This is because upriver settlements had to rely on steam power to be reached, whereas downriver settlements were able to take advantage of gravity. As river travel gave way to railroads and automobile traffic, the location along the stream did not matter as much, of course. Newer towns were born, and then died, along these transportation routes.

## *Louisiana Ghost Towns*

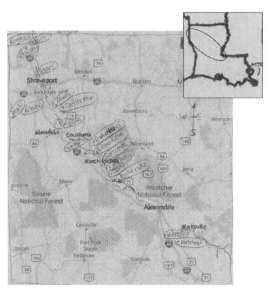

This tour begins south of Alexandria. You will drive north along the Red River through the Solomon Northrup Trail, the Cane River Creole National Heritage Trail, and into the northwestern Louisiana oil boom area. You will visit Meeker, Moorehead, Cloutierville, Derry / Magnolia, Melrose, St. Matthew, Bermuda / Oakland, Grand Ecore, Powhatan, Hanna, Caspiana, Gloster, Keachi, Taylortown, Mayers, Belcher, Hosston, Mira, and Rodessa.

As a French and Spanish colony, Louisiana developed as if it were in continental Europe — meaning, it had a few officially designated trading and religious centers, with farms and trading posts scattered throughout. Once it became American, Louisiana developed as an agricultural state that depended on the plantation system. The towns that were built to accommodate the plantation trade like

Shreveport, Marksville, Natchitoches, Alexandria, Le Compte, Coushatta, and Cheneyville, became very important to their communities, and they survived the railroad boom. That's not to say that all towns that existed prior to the Civil War hung on. Many, like Russelville and Red River Landing, diminished in the new social and economic climate of Reconstruction. Sadly, these communities did not leave visible traces.

Once it was admitted as a state in 1812, Louisiana became the destination for eastern planters wanting to exploit its good soil for secondary operations west of the Mississippi River. The plantations were built along bayous and creeks that drained into the Red River, as the main channel itself was prone to flooding, so its tributaries, often located on slightly higher ground, afforded some protection. These side waters include Bayou Boeuf, Bayou Robert, Bayou Pierre, Loggy Bayou, and Tone's Bayou. The self-sufficient plantations produced cash crops that were ferried down the rivers to large markets like Natchez, Baton Rouge, and New Orleans. The owners brought trade goods back and opened stores on their plantations that catered to community needs.

After freedom, the plantations witnessed major overhauls. The land was either sold and divided into smaller parcels or was converted into sharecropping holdings, and many of the original buildings were demolished or re-purposed. The ones that survived are often listed in maps as place names, like Red Chute (Bossier Parish) and East Point (Red River Parish). The plantation stores acted as trade and banking centers for farmers and sharecroppers, before the system gradually collapsed and better work, and educational opportunities, could be found in cities that grew with the railroads.

Many more "ghost towns" developed from the post-Civil War oil boom in northwestern Louisiana, when oil was discovered at the turn of the twentieth century north of Shreveport. Like the abrupt end of the plantation economy, the abrupt end to the oil boom allowed some towns to falter and others to weather the financial storm. The logging frenzy of the early twentieth century also produced a number of temporary saw mill towns, but traces of these hamlets have long been buzzed away (pun intended).

We'll start the journey along Bayou Boeuf.

### Meeker (Rapides Parish)

*What's to see:* Abandoned 1912 sugar mill

*How to get there:* Between Cheneyville and Lecompte on the western side of US 71. Turn west onto Sugarmill Road.

*Some history:* The plantations along Bayou Boeuf relied on sugarcane as their main cash crop. Before the Civil War, each plantation had its own processing plant, utilizing slave labor to extract the product and bring it to market, often by cutting paths to the bayou to load the goods onto flat-bottom boats. The little town of Meeker, named after a doctor, served several plantations around the bayou, but not much remains except a reminder of a more modern farming method - the imposing ruins of a sugarcane processing plant. The mill was built by Chicago investors in 1912 along the railroad line. In 1948, sugarcane farmers formed a cooperative and purchased the mill, squeezing their last cane in 1981.

*19.The old mill at Meeker, Rapides Parish.*

*The sights:* During its time in operation, the Meeker plant, a national registered historic place, was the northernmost sugar mill in the world. Today, it serves as the site of a chemical plant, but the façade and office buildings remain intact. You will only be able to visit it from outside a fenced perimeter, however, because it's an active industrial site and a security guard is on duty.

**By the way: The Solomon Northrup Trail**

Solomon Northrup has become a well-known figure in U.S. history thanks to his autobiographical book, Twelve Years a Slave, which recounted his kidnapping, enslavement, and eventual return to freedom from 1841 to 1853. Northrup's journey took him to Bayou Boeuf, a meandering arm of the Red River where sugar cane was the staple cash crop. He labored in brutal conditions, both from natural sources and human terror, and also explained the lifeways of men and women born and living within the dehumanizing conditions of chattel slavery. His story epitomized the threat of being "sold down the river" — the brutality of the anarchic lands west of the Mississippi River where profit overcame any scruples. In the late 1960s, researchers Dr. Sue Eakin and Dr. Joseph Logsdon retraced his route using the physical remains of the landscape, and by 1985, they established the Solomon Northrup Trail upon the publication of their guidebook. Today, the trail has been marked and mapped by the tourist commissions of Alexandria, Pineville, and Marksville so that motor tourists can witness Northrup's trek themselves.

*Side Note*: According to the Solomon Northrup Trail tour, the first Bowie Knife was commissioned at Rezin Bowie's plantation just north of Bunkie. However, the historic site/ghost town of Washington, Arkansas (see page 99) also claims to be the site of the first Bowie Knife commission by none other than Rezin's brother, James Bowie himself.

### Moorehead — Rosalie Pecan Plantation (Rapides Parish)

*What's to see:* Antebellum sugar mill

*How to get there:* From Meeker, drive north of Lecompte on US 71 to Moorehead. Turn northeast onto the Old Baton Rouge Highway, then turn east on Rosalie Road and follow it for about a mile. The mill is on the southern side of the road.

*Some history:* Moorehead lies in the heart of sugar cane country. The mill, built in the 1850s and modified for use over the decades, once belonged to the Rosalie Plantation, which now processes pecans instead of sugar. After the railroad arrived, the area was known as Moorland.

*The sights:* This mill, listed on the National Register of Historic Places, draws a good comparison to the modern one in Meeker. It is much smaller, made of brick, and has a dirt floor. The mill has a number of historically-minded supporters who occasionally stage special events inside to raise funds for upkeep.

### Cloutierville (Natchitoches Parish)

*What's to see:* A once bustling Main Street.

*How to get there:* From Alexandria, follow LA 1/ Bolton Avenue north past Boyce. You will continue on LA 1 for about 50 miles to Cloutierville. The town itself sits along LA 495 just north of LA 1.

20.*The Carnahan Store in Cloutierville, Natchitoches Parish, in 1940 (LOC).*

*Some history:* Cloutierville is a text-book example of an antebellum settlement. Founded as a plantation settlement in 1822, Cloutierville does not have a downtown. Instead, its houses and businesses hug both sides of the road, which parallels the Cane River — for many years, its main source of transportation and connection to the outside world. A few old, derelict buildings can be seen in the town, and its large and historic cemetery is worth an extended visit. Kate Chopin, author of *The Awakening,* once resided here, but the family's mansion was destroyed by vandals. When I last visited it, a feral hog rooted among the charred house remains in the front yard. In 2018, Cloutierville's school closed, thus cementing its status as Louisiana's newest ghost town.

*21.Livingston Grocers in Cloutierville, Natchitoches Parish still stands.*

*The sights:* All of the sights in Cloutierville can be visited along the LA 495. The former bank building, the silent cotton gin, defunct service stations, and a few empty grocery stores hint at the town's former busy existence. While not much goes on in the town anymore, many people still consider Cloutierville home. Their hometown pride is evident in the annual Mardi Gras parade.

*22.Cloutierville's former bank building was built in 1919.*

**Derry — Magnolia Plantation (Natchitoches Parish)**

*What's to see:* A fairly intact plantation and early twentieth century commercial buildings.

*How to get there:* From Alexandria, follow LA 1/Bolton Avenue north past Boyce. You will continue on LA 1 for about 50 miles until just past Cloutierville. Then, you will turn north onto LA 119 and follow it briefly to the Magnolia Plantation in Derry.

*Some history:* Derry is home to the famous Magnolia Plantation, founded in 1753 and still owned and operated by the original family. The plantation's cotton crops surpassed any other in Louisiana until the Civil War, and its main house was occupied, then burned, by federal troops in 1864. Like most plantations west of the Mississippi River, the plantation was not run by the family, but rather by a hired overseer whose job was to subjugate the enslaved people and keep detailed records of the production. After freedom, the slave cabins, made of brick formed from the clay beds along the Red River, became the homes of sharecroppers. One of the cabins was converted into a school, but eventually, the children attended a larger school up the road at St. James. While for a long time, the plantation operated like its own insular village, the small community of Derry established itself after the Civil War to provide commercial services to the area's rural inhabitants.

*The sights:* Derry has a number of abandoned gas stations but without much architectural interest. To see some really old places, a visit to the Magnolia Plantation is warranted. Except for the "big house," which was rebuilt in 1890 and is home to the planter family, all of the plantation's buildings are maintained and interpreted by the National Park Service and are open for self-guided tours. This includes several brick cabins that served as a slave, then sharecropper's quarters, as well an eighteenth-century blacksmith shop, an early twentieth century cotton gin, and a nineteenth century overseer's house. Upon close inspection, many ancient artifacts can be discovered on the dirt floor of the blacksmith shop, but please note that as a protected site, any collecting is off-limits.

*23.Brick cabin at the Magnolia Plantation in Derry, Natchitoches Parish.*

### Melrose (Natchitoches Parish)

*What's to see:* Small strip of commercial buildings and a plantation.

*How to get there*: Go north on LA 119 from the Magnolia Plantation to Melrose. As this road is a part of the Cane River Creole National Historic District, signs to Melrose are clearly marked.

*Some history:* Like many of the small places that line the banks of the Red River, Melrose was the center of an antebellum plantation that, after freedom, became a commercial center for a post office, a store, and juke joints. The little hamlet is named after the impressive Melrose Plantation, which was built in 1796 in the French Creole style by Louis Metoyer, son of Marie Therese Coincoin, after he received a Spanish land grant.

*24.Street scene in 1940's Melrose, Natchitoches Parish (LOC).*

*The sights:* The small town of Melrose has a few shuttered, mid- twentieth century store fronts and gas stations. Melrose Plantation, which is owned and run by the Association of Natchitoches Women for the Preservation of Historic Natchitoches, provides tours. The plantation is home to the "African House," a small, brick outbuilding with an incredibly impressive roof structure. Metoyer had the structure built by enslaved people who, most likely, originated directly from Congo. Inside the one-room, two story building is a wall mural painted by Clementine Hunter, the daughter of a sharecropper who worked as a cook at the plantation in the first half of the twentieth century. There is no other building like the African House in the entire North American continent.

## By the way: Cane River Creoles

Just outside of Melrose lies the oldest church in Louisiana founded by free people of color, the Metoyer family. To get there, go southwest on LA 493. You will cross the Cane River; immediately turn south onto LA 484 to get to the church.

In 1826, the children of Marie Therese Coincoin established the catholic St. Augustine Church and cemetery at Isle Brevelle, an insular inlet along the bayous by the Red River. Marie Therese (1742-1816) was an enslaved woman of French, African, and Indian descent who endured two imposed relationships by slave owners that led to several children. Marie Therese, whose parents named her Coincoin to remind her of her Old World roots, was branded a prostitute by the parish priest even though as an enslaved person, she could never have consented to sexual relationships. The last relationship, with Pierre Metoyer, led to her freedom and that of their children in 1787. Metoyer deeded land to her soon thereafter, and she established her own plantation and cattle ranch. With the money she made as a planter and noted healer, Marie Therese Coincoin was able to buy her older children from her first relationship and freed them, too. Marie Therese's children formed the nucleus of the French-African Creole families along the Cane River, who then established the St. Augustine church, free from cruel judgement. The Metoyers married other Creole families, maintained their French- African- Caribbean language and customs, and created an identity separate and cloistered from the American influence that appeared after

1803. Today, the community is part of Cane River Creole National Heritage Area.

### St. Matthew (Natchitoches Parish)

*What's to see:* A large, abandoned high school.

*ow to get there:* From Melrose, continue following LA 119 north to St. Matthew School, which will be on the west side of the road.

*Some history:* The school was initially founded in 1916 by the local Baptist church to provide high school education to rural African American and Creole children. Enrollment grew so much that in 1952, a modern, brick building opened. The school remained unofficially segregated until court orders in the 1980s led to the consolidation of school districts throughout Louisiana. Students were bused into Natchitoches, and the St. Matthew school closed in 1989.

*The sights:* The cavernous high school is quickly decaying in the wet atmosphere along the Cane River bayous. Behind the school are cement foundations of other buildings. There is also a quaint Baptist church, complete with an interesting, above-ground cemetery.

### Bermuda, Oakland Plantation (Natchitoches Parish)

*What's to see:* Intact plantation and headquarters of the Cane River Creole National Historic District.

*How to get there:* Go north on LA 119 to the Oakland Plantation. Follow the signs to the parking lot behind the plantation.

*Some history:* Once known as Bermuda, the Oakland Plantation complex developed from a Spanish land grant in 1789. The Prudhomme family planted cotton, and grew the operation into its own village, complete with *pigeonnieres* — they raised and ate pigeons. In all of its years of existence, the plantation never suffered a major fire, nor was it destroyed during the Civil War. Therefore, all of the buildings are original to the grounds and depict an intact, insular plantation world. The National Park Service, which maintains the buildings on the premises, keeps the home in its 1960's condition, which is when the grounds were donated to the government for education and preservation.

25.*Oakland's bottle garden in Natchitoches Parish is must-see for gardeners.*

*The sights:* The grounds of the Oakland Plantation reflect deep cultural history. The "big house" is built in the Creole style with a raised foundation, heavy timbers, large wrap-around porch, and a pitched roof. Beneath the porch is an entire work area, where enslaved people could escape from the heat; however, here is also where they could be placed in chains as punishment and where some of the household slaves slept at night. The outbuildings are constructed with timber chinked with *bousillage*, a mixture of clay and plant fibers. The overseer house and former slave cabins, which became sharecropper homes after the Civil War, sport generations of paint, newspaper used as wall paper, and family photographs. Park employees and volunteers provide very detailed and insightful tours. Don't miss the oak alley in the front of the plantation home, as well as the garden beds lined with two hundred years' worth of wine bottles.

**By the way: El Camino de Real and Los Adaes**

When the French set up a fort in the Natchitoches village in 1714, the Spanish decided to erect their own fort to lay claim to western portions of the Red River Valley. Between 1716 and 1720, they built the mission and presidio called San Miguel de Linares de los Adaes, which centered on an Adaen village (related to the Caddos) and sat just ten miles from the French Fort Natchitoche. Los Adaes not only became the capital of Spanish Texas, but was also the end station of the Camino de Real, or Royal Road, that began at Guerrero (Coahuila). After the Spanish took control of Louisiana Territory after the French Indian Wars in 1763, the government extended the road into Natchitoches. Today, tourists can see original traces of the route between Natchitoches and the mission of Los Adaes, which is a Louisiana State Historic Site.

**By the way: Grand Ecore**

North of Natchitoches is the old town of Grand Ecore. Named after the high bluff that overlooks the Red River, the location was a steamboat portage and stage coach stop on the road to Shreveport before the Civil War. While the town is no longer around, the bluff is saturated with history. At eighty feet, it is a prominent feature in this otherwise flat region, serving as a landmark for Spanish and French explorers and settlers. The Grand Ecore is the reason why Natchitoches exists, as it shielded the settlement from major floods. The bluff allowed Natchitoches to become a head of navigation for the lower Red River, as above the bluff lay the confusing bayous of the Great Raft. During the Civil War, Confederate troops built entrenchments here in order to defend their location from the Union flotilla during the Red River Campaign of 1864. The Grand Ecore visitor's center, located off LA 6 north of Natchitoches, explains the Red River and the bluff in great detail, and the views are wonderful. A trace of the Jefferson Highway (see page 124) can be driven along a dead-end street across the highway from the Grand Ecore visitor's center.

### Powhatan (Natchitoches Parish)

*What's to see:* Some derelict buildings and some restored places.

*How to get there:* From Natchitoches, follow LA 1 north to Powhatan.

*Some history:* Powhatan owes its existence to the Texas and Pacific Railway, which founded the town along this line in the early twentieth century. The town built up along the tracks and has a very narrow, long footprint. While the trains still pass, they no longer stop in the town, and school children are bussed to neighboring districts.

*The sights:* Powhatan sports a series of abandoned commercial buildings that dot its main road, which fittingly enough is called Railroad Street. To the north on LA 1, you will find a few restored railroad era buildings that once belonged to Powhatan but are now in the hands of preservationists.

### Hanna (Red River Parish)

*What's to see:* A school.

*How to get there:* Hanna lies north of Powhatan on LA 1.

*Some history:* Hanna was once the site of a major Caddo village, now called the Gahagan site, which the tribe inhabited over one thousand years ago. Hanna itself was founded when the railroad came through in the 1880s. Today, the little town is also a port on the J. Bennett Johnston Waterway, the commercial traffic arm of the Red River. With all of this activity, one would think that Hanna is a burgeoning town, but most of its inhabitants have moved to Shreveport, Coushatta, or Natchitoches.

26. *The school in Hanna (Red River Parish) is supposed to be haunted, of course.*

*The sights:* The only remainder of note in Hanna is its two-story, brick school, built in the 1930s. Two side doors segregated the boys from the girls. Its solid construction tells of a formerly prosperous railroad town. The school is inaccessible and can only be appreciated from the road.

## By the way: The Great Red River Raft

The landscape north of Natchitoches reveals itself as flat and water logged. This is because the area used to be inundated with bayous and lakes formed by the Great Red River Raft, an immense log jam over one hundred miles in length and at times, fifty miles wide. Caddos, French, and Spanish governments noted the natural dams, or "rafts," that clogged up the Red River, but simply accepted it as part of the natural landscape.

*27.Woodruff's raft clearing in 1873 (State Library of Louisiana).*

After 1803, Americans treated the raft as an impediment to commerce that needed to be removed. In 1832, river boat captain Henry Shreve won the contract to remove the first log jam just north of Natchitoches. He even patented his own snag boat to help his crew in this task.

However, by 1837, the U.S. found itself mired in the first Great Depression, which cut short continued funding for the raft clearing. The raft reappeared north of Shreveport (founded in 1836) in the ensuing 40 years until 1873, when the Army Corps of Engineers cleared and dynamited the last raft.

### Caspiana (Caddo Parish)

*What's to see:* An abandoned roadside store.

*How to get there:* Continue north on LA 1 for ten miles to get to Caspiana.

*28.The Hutchinson store in Caspiana, Caddo Parish.*

*Some history:* The little hamlet of Caspiana is named after the Caspiana Plantation, which was founded by the Hutchinson family in 1852. The original "big house" was donated to the Pioneer Heritage Center at Louisiana State University in 1977; the current house, built in 1910, is a wedding venue. Like all other operating plantations in the region, Caspiana became home to a number of sharecropping families after the Civil War, all of whom frequented plantation stores to buy their groceries and seeds. These stores were always operated by the plantation-owning family, who would pay the sharecroppers in scrip that could only be cashed in at their own stores. This practice not only kept the wealth (both financial and labor) inside the planter class, but also retarded the economic development of the entire region.

*The sights*: The roadside store, which closed in the 1980s, dates from the turn of the twentieth century and served travelers along LA 1. This store is not to be confused with the Caspiana Planation Store, which was built in 1906 and moved to Natchitoches to be preserved in 1991. The on-site store, once owned by members of the Hutchinson family, is not accessible except from the outside but as of this writing, still sports the unleaded and leaded gasoline dispensers.

### Gloster (DeSoto Parish)

*What's to see*: Several early twentieth century buildings, and nineteenth century plantation homes.

*How to get there*: Just north of Caspiana is Ellerbe Road. Turn west on Ellerbe until it intersects with LA 175, then turn south onto LA 175. Follow LA 175 to Kingston. At Kingston, turn west onto LA 5 and follow the road into Gloster.

*Some history*: Gloster grew as a town to support area plantations, including Roseneath (late 1840s) and Myrtle Hill (1852). The Texas and Pacific Railway cut its path through the town, but the rail line has been abandoned.

*The sights*: Little Gloster sports three houses, all antebellum, on the National Register: Myrtle Hill, Roseneath, and the deteriorating Thomas Scott House. All three are privately owned. Roseneath has gained a lot of attention over the years because its exterior has been used for a TV show about vampires, the HBO series *Trueblood*. Several commercial buildings, some abandoned, line the streets in Gloster.

### Keachi (DeSoto Parish)

*What's to see*: Several historically significant antebellum commercial structures, homes and churches — ten of which are listed on the National Register; a Confederate cemetery; and an abandoned school. Please note that the spelling of the town is disputed: depending on the source, it has been spelled Keatchi, Keachie, or Keechi.

*How to get there*: From Gloster, follow LA 5 west past Kickapoo to Keachi.

*29.An antebellum store in Keachi, DeSoto Parish.*

*Some history*: As town histories go, Keachi, named after a Caddoan tribe, incorporated very early – it was considered a legitimate town by 1852, with a post office, several churches, a general store, and a Masonic Lodge. In 1856, the Keachi Female Seminary, a Baptist institution, opened to cater to the daughters from the surrounding plantations. The college remained an important institution until 1912. During the Civil War, the college acted as a hospital to tend those wounded during the battles at Mansfield and Pleasant Hill. Some of the Confederate soldiers who did not survive the confrontation are buried at the Confederate Cemetery (while soldiers were generally buried en-masse because of their lack of identification, the graveyards separated Confederate from Union burials. Most Union causalities were repatriated to their company's home turfs.) Keachi was able to weather modernization during the post-war economy when the train came through, and continued operating as a town for decades afterwards. Luckily, it never suffered a major fire, leaving its ante-bellum, Greek Revival structures intact. The town's public high school was shuttered upon integration in the 1980s. Keachi students were consolidated into the North Desoto school district.

*30. The old school in Keachi (DeSoto Parish) is best seen in winter when the trees are bare.*

*The sights*: Among the plethora of architectural treasures, the most astonishing building in Keachi is its old mercantile, which has a grand, plantation-like façade and, without a whitewash, the gray wood gives it a definite haunted look. Originally built in 1850 and operated as the Fullilove General Store (the Fulliloves also owned a plantation), it was bought by the Nelson family, whose name is still on the front of the store. Next door to the mercantile is the town's Masonic Lodge, built in 1880. To the west of the mercantile are a few antebellum homes. On the north side sit the remains of an attempt to recreate the Keachi Female Seminary building. While the structure looks dilapidated, it is not a contemporary of the original building, save for the bell. Behind the building is the abandoned, two story high school. Follow LA 5 west a bit more to get to the Confederate Cemetery. The quaint ante-bellum churches for the Presbyterian and Methodist congregations sit along LA 5 east of the mercantile. The large Fullilove-Schuler-Cathy home (named after the Cathy family, which sold Ford automobiles in Keachi) sits south of the mercantile. Originally built as a dog trot cabin in the early 1850s, inhabitants had it enlarged over the years so that it is now a rambling home owned and maintained by the Keachi Historical Society.

**By the way: The Mansfield Battle of 1864**

South of the Desoto Parish seat of Mansfield is the site of the definitive battle for the Trans-Mississippi region during the Civil War. In 1864, Admiral Porter of the U.S. navy brought iron clads, tin clads, and gun boats up the Red River above Natchitoches in the hopes of invading Shreveport, but his fleet was turned back by Confederate defense fortifications at the Grand Ecore. At the same time, General Banks of the U.S. Army marched several thousand troops towards the road into Shreveport. On his journey northwest, he encountered Confederate troops, led under Confederate General Taylor, just south of Mansfield. The Confederate Army, mostly comprised of Louisianans, Texans, and Arkansans, forced Banks's army into a full retreat, engaging them twice more further south at Pleasant Hill. After the battle, most of the casualties were carried to the Female Academy in Mansfield (101 Monroe Street), where a parking lot hides the pit that holds the soldiers' amputated limbs. Today, the battle site, which sits just south of Mansfield on the old stage coach road (LA 175), can be toured through a very informative interpretive center.

### Taylortown (Bossier Parish)

*What's to see*: An abandoned church tower.

*How to get there*: From Keachi, go east on LA 5 to US 171. Turn south on US 171 and follow it through Grand Cane into Mansfield. In Mansfield, turn east onto Polk Street/ US 84 and follow it for 14 miles to the Red River at Grand Bayou. At Grand Bayou, turn south on US 84/ LA 1 to Armistead. There, turn east onto US 84/US 371 and drive to Coushatta. Once you cross the Red River, turn northeast onto US 371/ LA 179/ Ringgold Avenue. Continue following this street north of Coushatta, then turn northwest onto US 71. Drive about 30 miles north to Taylortown. The church tower sits along US 71 in a field and is not easily visible or accessible from the road.

*Some history:* Originally part of larger plantation systems called Elm Grove, Waterloo, and Ash Point, Taylortown grew into a sizeable community after the Civil War when the railroad built its tracks through town and featured at least one cotton gin, several stores, a Masonic Lodge, and impressive church buildings. In 1921, its school was consolidated into the Elm Grove School, and the town slowly dwindled in significance. The last remaining structure from the original town is the bell tower that belonged to the 1898 Methodist Church. According to legend, the bell tower is haunted by a jilted bride. Like with all ghost stories, a kernel of truth emerges with some research. In 1905, Lucille Mercer, the young daughter of the owner of Elm Grove Plantation, died a week before her wedding. Her grief-stricken family wrote a beautiful tribute to her in the *Bossier Banner*:

*Dressed in bridal robes of softest lace,*
*She lay with gentle upturned face;*
*A look of calmest peace was there,*
*For God had taken her into His care.*
*She seemed a lovely recumbent statue,*
*Lying there in a the snow-white casket,*
*And we know that God in His Great love*
*Had taken her to His home above.*
*With tearful eyes we knelt and gazed*
*Upon that face of matchless grace,*
*For upon it God had set His seal,*
*That she was His for future years.*
*Though our hearts are broken in twain,*
*Lucille, you have not died in vain;*

*We shall come to you in your celestial home,*
*Where God will claim us, too, as His own.*
*Lucille, dear heart, we loved you so,*
*And it was hard, so hard, to have you go.*
*Yet, we would not have you back again*
*In this weary world of trials and pains.*
*And now, a last long farewell, dear heart,*
*For we know that we must part,*
*And leave you lying in Death's cold embrace –*
*With the look of rapture on your face –*
*For you have only gone one before*
*To prepare a place for your loved ones here below,*
*And we shall surely remember your prayer,*
*To meet you in eternity.*

*31.The last remain of old Taylortown sits in a field.*

*The sights*: The bell tower is the only extant remainder of the church and is in situ in a corn field. It sits behind the railroad tracks. For the best view, turn east onto LA 527 and follow the south fence row.

**By the way: The Jefferson Highway**

Once you drive on US 71, you are also driving on the federalized portion of the Jefferson Highway. Named after the nation's third president, this road began in 1916 as a National Auto Trail, funded by both bicycle and car enthusiasts. In 1926, the federal government created the national highway systems, and US 71 replaced portions of the 1916 route. The Jefferson Auto Trail was known as the "Palm to Pine Highway" because it stretched from New Orleans to Winnipeg, Manitoba, Canada. Taylortown sits on the original alignment of the 1926 road (the 1916 road parallels the Red River to the west and is partially designated today as LA 1).

*32.The calaboose from Mayers (Bossier Parish) hides behind a fence.*

**Mayers (Bossier Parish)**

*What's to see*: A calaboose.

*How to get there*: Continue driving north on US 71 until it intersects with LA 612. At the northwestern corner of this intersection is the lone remains of Mayers.

*Some history*: The town lies now beneath fields, but before it succumbed to industrialized agriculture, it housed a cotton gin and a few stores. Its purpose was to serve the nearby Scopena Plantation.

*The sights*: The old Louisiana Railway and Navigation Line (later, the Kansas City Southern Railway) is littered with settlements that grew and diminished with the rails. Mayers is unique in that it still sports its old jail. Otherwise, there's nothing here to indicate that a town had once formed here. Mayers isn't even on maps anymore.

### Belcher – Belcher Mound (Caddo Parish)

*What's to see*: Caddo mounds, but on private property.

*How to get there*: In downtown Shreveport, go north on US 71/ LA 1 / Spring Street. About two miles north from the city center, turn east on Hearne Avenue, then turn north onto LA 3049/ Grimmett Drive. Follow LA 3049/ Grimmett Drive north for about 16 miles to Belcher.

*Some history*: Belcher itself is not a ghost town, but rather a pin-neat farming community with a real Louisiana quaintness. However, to its east is the site of a large Caddo settlement and mound complex. Clarence H. Webb, a pediatrician who devoted his spare time to the study of archeology, excavated the village in the 1960s. There, he and his team found evidence of a sophisticated agricultural settlement that utilized the land at the Red River to grow crops, fish, and build burial mounds. The site was occupied by Caddoans until either just before or just after European exploration. Old Caddoan villages, belonging mainly to the

Kadohadacho tribe of the Caddos, dot the landscapes of northwestern Louisiana and southwestern Arkansas.

*The sights*: A plantation (north of town on LA 3049) is built on top of a series of seven mounds, which may have held the homes, then burial places, of Caddo chieftains. A helpful historical marker on the side of the road provides more information.

**By the way: American Plantation Row**

As you travel on LA 3049 (also called the Dixie to Shreveport Highway), you will see many plantation sites. These are Anglo-American plantations that developed after Shreveport became a major port city in 1837; before that year, most of the plantations in Louisiana's Red River Valley were confined to the stream from Natchitoches southward, since the Great Raft (see page 70) made transport and navigation difficult. Texas Street in Shreveport intersects with the Grand Tour in *Traveling History with Bonnie and Clyde*.

**Hosston (Caddo Parish)**

*What's to see:* A semi-abandoned downtown.

*How to get there*: From Belcher, travel northwest on LA 530 to US 71. Turn north onto US 71 and follow it through Gilliam (see page 82) into Hosston.

*Some history*: Hosston is the name given to the town after the railroad came through. Originally, it was known as Hale or Hale Town. Established in the 1840s by a man named Hale who worked as an overseer for the large and brutal Robert Hamilton plantation, the little settlement centered an isolated portion of Caddo Parish, set among bogs and bayous. Today, the town still hangs on, with a branch of the Caddo Parish Public Library still open half of the week. *The sights:* Hosston's downtown sports a number of ruins in its former commercial district on Parkway Drive (the original alignment of US 71) and Magnolia Street. One of the buildings was fairly recently turned into an antique store/museum that focuses on commercial artifacts that reference African American history and cultural treatment. The former public school was built in 1931. It became an alternative school before it closed permanently in 2012. The building is now a community center.

*33.Downtown Hosston, Caddo Parish.*

**By the way: Red River Crossroads Museum**

The Red River Crossroads Historical & Cultural Association runs the North Caddo Museum in the library in Gilliam (Caddo Parish), and it is well worth the stop. Outside displays explain cotton farming in the period after the Civil War, and inside exhibits detail early inhabitants and oil discoveries in northwest Louisiana.

## Mira (Caddo Parish)

*What's to see:* An old commercial building and a modern but abandoned church.

*How to get there*: From Hosston, travel north on US 71 to Mira.

*Some history*: Mira was once a small town on the Texas and Pacific Railway. It grew into a village after the removal of the second raft in 1873, which cleared the swampy lands. Oil and gas discoveries, as well as cotton growing and cattle ranching, help the town prosper with cotton gins, wagon yards, and boarding houses. However, prosperity bred violence.

Caddo Parish, and the towns in the northwestern section in particular, witnessed exceptional brutality against African Americans. The rate of homicides committed by white men against black men was the highest in the postwar era South during the last quarter of the twentieth century. According to historian Gilles Vandal, thirty percent of the parish's white population participated in lynchings against blacks (execution-style murder of a person by a group of people without legal authority) in Caddo Parish. Over three-quarters of the murderers stemmed from the planter classes. While the white capitalists blamed the lynchings on disputes between black men, attitudes shifted when Charles Tyson, a prominent preacher from nearby Myrtis, was hanged in a tree in the area in 1913. A grand jury convened in Shreveport to investigate the crime, which was a rare justice-seeking mission in this period. While the jury did not discuss any named perpetrators, it acknowledged that the murder had been perpetrated by white men and it strongly condemned "the bloodthirsty men" who "should not be countenanced in this age of enlightenment." (*Times-Picayune,* March 6, 1913). However, even with this grand-standing, the grand jury didn't level any direct accusations. Most of the murders committed by white men on black men and women in northwestern Louisiana remain unsolved.

*The sights*: A modern, red bricked church sits abandoned along the highway strip of what used to be Mira. A few stores remain open, but an early twentieth century commercial building is overgrown. On top of its flat roof one can discern the message "MIRA → 8" if viewed from an air plane. This was a way-marker, which helped pilots find their way around the area during the early aviation era.

34.*Ghost town hunters can locate Mira from their vintage flying machines (Google).*

## Rodessa (Caddo Parish)

*What's to see*: Fantastic old school and lots of commercial ruins.

*How to get there*: Just north of Mira is the Mira-Myrtis Road. Turn west on this road and follow it to LA 1. Drive north on LA 1 to reach Rodessa.

*Some history*: Surveyors in northwestern Caddo Parish described the land as mosquito-infested and impassable, with unbearably hot summers. This may be why there was not much settlement activity until after the Civil War, when the Great Raft (see page 70) was removed. Several African American families founded farms and sharecropped in the area, and the road names reflect their legacies: Tyson and Hale, for example (there were white and black families of the name, with many interrelated lineages). Rodessa, originally called Frog Level but renamed when the Kansas City Southern laid tracks through town in 1898, was founded during an oil boom. By 1940, the Rodessa Patch had produced over 117 million barrels of oil. None of the prosperity remained in the town, however. Though the wealth had built permanent infrastructure, when the oil fields dried up, so did the influx of cash. A tornado that killed twenty people in 1938 didn't help matters. Today, Rodessa, with its commercial strip and very imposing, abandoned high school, is slowly but surely decaying.

*The sights:* The water tower is surrounded by a park on which commercial buildings used to sit. Along one of the walls is a mural that harks back to prosperous times. At the corner of Front Street and Pennock Street is a line of commercial buildings with "no trespassing" signs. Across the tracks from the post office sits the town's Masonic Lodge. Drive a bit further east to encounter the imposing but abandoned high school. Its impressive rock edifice is slowly rotting, so take caution of falling debris.

This is the end of Louisiana's Red River Valley Ghost Town Tour!

To begin the Arkansas journey of ghost towns, go east on Rodessa's Main Street, aka LA 168 aka The Rodessa-Ida Road, to Ida. Don't miss visiting the 1910 calaboose once you enter Ida, which sits at the corner of Magnolia and Louisiana Streets. To drive into Arkansas, go north on Louisiana Street / US 71.

# Arkansas Ghosts Towns

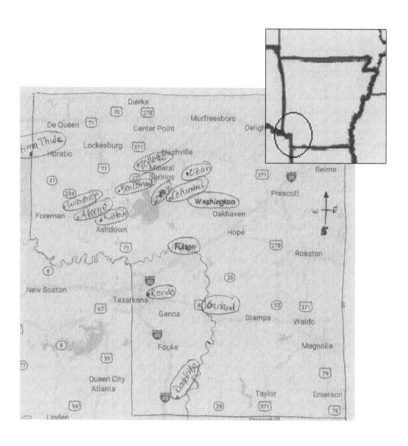

The tour runs from the south to the north to the west, following the Great Bend of the Red River. You will visit Doddridge, Rondo, Garland City, Fulton, Washington, Ozan, Columbus, Okay, Tollette, Ben Lomand, Wilton, Alleene, Winthrop, and Ultima Thule.

Depending on the culture, settlement patterns in the Great Bend region differed greatly. The Caddoans saw the area as a perfect place to center their civilization; according to their origin story, the Caddoans emerged from Boyd Hill in today's Lafayette County. Thus, the Great Bend was well populated before the Europeans arrived, with farming compounds and mound complexes built around large corn fields that hugged oxbow lakes. When American settlers arrived after the Louisiana Purchase, they noted the immense number of mounds up and down the Red River. One can argue that the entire area is actually a Caddoan ghost town.

European settlers treated the region as a conduit. The Spanish slashed and burned their way from the Mississippi River to Texas. The French simply established trading posts. For the Americans, the Great Bend of the Red River served as a thoroughfare into Texas. The Texas Road, now known as the "Great Southwest Trail," has been named in historical accounts as the Chihuahua Trail and (partly) as Trammel's Trace. It was along this road where the Choctaws and Chickasaws moved into Indian Territory, and where some of Stephen F. Austin's "Original 300" walked, as the first legitimate American *empresario*, into Texas.

Some settlers stayed in the region, of course, and like in Louisiana, economic activity dictated their colonization. While there were many plantations, small-scale farms tended to predominate, and the timber industry became a very important economic engine as well.

We'll start the journey at the Louisiana/Arkansas border and work our way north, then northwest.

## Doddridge (Miller County)

*What's to see:* A cute little downtown and the preserved hulk of the last ferry to cross the Red River.

*How to get there:* Doddridge sits just west of the intersection of US 71 and AR 160 in southern Miller County, about eight miles north of the Louisiana border.

*Some history:* Doddridge was a town built upon the introduction of the Texas and Pacific Railway, but its origins are much older than that. The community is not far away from Spring Bank, an old planation landing for several cotton growers in the pre-Civil War era. At the turn of the nineteenth century, the Sulphur River Indian Factory (Caddo Agency) sat where the Sulphur River enters into the Red River. It was here where the Caddos of the Great Bend region signed away their territorial claims to the United States in exchange for a small annuity and promised lands further west, although at this point, there weren't any lands designated to them for distribution. In the 1890s, a coal mining community aptly named Black Diamond developed nearby, as did some oil fields by the 1940s. Doddridge's best claim to fame, though, is its ties to the Spring Bank ferry. From 1834 until 1995, people crossed the Red River on a contraption that through the years used pulleys, oars, gasoline, and finally, diesel. The erection of the AR 160 bridge signaled the end of the last ferry on the Red River.

*The sights*: Downtown Doddridge has a number of vacant buildings, including one that houses a museum (when a volunteer is able to open it). Across the street from the commercial strip are more overgrown buildings as well as the well-preserved hulk of the actual, last Spring Bank Ferry. Visiting the remains of this important industrial artifact is a pilgrimage every Red River historian should take.

### Rondo (Miller County)

*What's to see:* A large cemetery.

*How to get there*: From Doddridge, go north on US 71 through Fouke (Home of the Bog Monster) and follow all the way into Texarkana. In downtown Texarkana, turn west on US 82/ US 67/ 9th Street, then follow US 67/ Broad street north when it splits. Follow US 67 for about a mile, then turn east onto 19th street/ Old Post road. Follow 19th street /McClure road street to the Rondo Cemetery at the intersection with Cobb Lane.

*Some history*: Throughout its existence, Rondo was considered an outpost for the United States. Located west of the Red River in disputed territory — was it in Texas? Arkansas? Indian Territory? — the little community of planters, mostly bachelor men, saw its first building, the Masonic Hall, erected in 1818. About twenty years later, the community grew into an actual town with general stores, gins and church buildings. Named after a dice game, Rondo saw its future secured when the road into town was designated for mail and stage coaches. During the Civil War, this road proved fortuitous, as the Confederate government moved its archives from Washington to Rondo to avoid their destruction by the Union army. The coming of the railroads doomed Rondo, however. When the Cairo and Fulton Railroad (originally, the St. Louis, Iron Mountain, and Southern Railway) laid its route, it chose to profit from building town sites of its own rather than linking to the present towns. Texarkana and Hope became the shiny new "railroad cities" and left historic places like Rondo behind.

*38.Rondo's cemetery gate was built by the WPA in 1933.*

*The sights*: There isn't much to see in Rondo except for the impressive cemetery with several old graves, including mass graves of unknown Texas Confederate volunteers who died from either cholera, typhoid, or measles outbreaks. The old chapel, built in the 1930s, has now caved in, and the caretaker's cottage has also been razed. The cemetery's gate was built by the Civilian Conservation Corps in the 1933.

## By the way: Dooley's Ferry

Just north of the Rondo cemetery is the Old Post Road/ Stagecoach Road. In the 1830s, when the road was blazed, it linked Rondo to Dooley's Ferry at the Red River. Travel along the road to the west bank of Dooley's Ferry is still possible, but neither the ferry crossing, nor even a bridge that replaced the ferry, exist anymore. Confederates built an earthen fortification on the east bank of the crossing to halt a possible Union invasion. The mounds of the earth works can still be discerned in some areas on the eastern side of Dooley's Ferry Road in Lafayette County.

## Garland City (Miller County)

*What's to see*: A few commercial buildings that have seen better days and an abandoned school.

*How to get there*: From Rondo, drive south on AR 237/ N. Rondo Road to the intersection with US 82/ 9th Street. Turn east on US 82/ 9th Street and follow it to Garland. Turn south on AR 134 to see the school at the intersection of AR 134 and Lowe Street. Follow AR 134 to N. Wilson Street, then turn north on N. Wilson Street. Turn southeast onto Front Street to get to the remains of downtown Garland. To see the Red River, go north on N. Wilson Street and then, turn east onto US 82. A small park/boat landing is available at the shore of the river.

*Some history*: Garland City (or simply Garland) was founded in 1833 as a ferry crossing and steam boat landing after the first clearing of the Red River Raft down river by Natchitoches. It grew into a fairly important town that separated Miller from Lafayette County. The St. Louis and Southwestern Railway crossed the Red River in Garland by the turn of the twentieth century, ensuring its continued survival even with the many floods the town experienced over the years. In the 1920s, the town petitioned for a road bridge to be built over the Red River on the Texarkana to Magnolia Road (US 82), and the state began construction in 1927. On the morning of September 3, 1930, the almost-completed Garland City bridge was wracked by a blast that propelled the newly-built span into the Red River. The

*39.Downtown Garland City, Miller County*

privately-operated Kansas City Bridge Company rebuilt the span with the promise of being able to charge tolls. The State of Arkansas ended up charging two construction workers with the crime, but charges were dismissed when the men presented alibis. Locals spoke amongst themselves that it may have been the ferry operator who organized the blast, as he had been vocally protesting the bridge's erection. The new truss bridge opened in 1931, but was demolished fifty years later when US 82 was straightened and the new bridge bypassed the town by several hundred feet.

*The sights*: Vey few commercial buildings sit along Front Street, though the grain silos directly across the street from the remaining commercial strip provide a certain ambience. The former school has two entrances, one for girls and one for boys, and was at one time used as a community center.

40.The Pennsylvania Truss at Garland City carried US 82
*before a new bridge was built in 1981 (LOC).*

### By the way: Boyd Hill

Northeast of Garland sits a 390 ft elevation called Boyd Hill. In 1806, two Caddoan guides, Cut Finger and Grand Ozages, told Peter Custis and Thomas Freeman during the Red River expedition that according to legend, this mountain constituted the birthplace of the Caddo people. Boyd Hill is still in a fairly natural state, with cypress trees, boulders, and small streams of water. Thought it's on private property, the hill lies next to a county road so that it can be fairly easily viewed. To get to Boyd Hill from Garland City, go east on US 82, then north on CR 5. Follow CR 5 into the community of Boyd Hill, and travel north on CR 104 (improved but unpaved). Boyd Hill is unmarked, but it's not difficult to discern on the east side of the road, despite the undergrowth surrounding the it.

### Fulton (Hempstead County)

*What's to see*: A storied train bridge over the Red River, the Great Bend of the Red River, and sparse remains of the downtown.

*41.Fulton's busy intersection of the railroad and river in the early 20th century (AHA).*

*How to get there:* From Garland, return to Texarkana by driving US 82 to the west. In Texarkana, turn northeast onto US 67/ Broad Street and follow it for about twenty miles to Fulton. Turn north on AR 355 just after the Red River Bridge, then turn southwest onto Ina Street to see the railroad bridge. Continue on Ina Street as it winds its way into Little River Street, which was once Fulton's Main Street.

*Some history*: Fulton began life in 1819 as a town-creation scheme led by several investors. At first a ferry crossing into Spanish Texas, it became a steam boat landing by the 1830s, and quickly was considered "one of the most important river towns on the Red River... the gateway to the Southwest" (*Arkansas Gazette*). Hotels, boarding houses, saloons, gambling halls, general stores, and moonshiners gave Fulton a measure of commercial success. Many people came through Fulton on their way into Texas, including the "Original 300" settlers of Austin's Colony into Mexican Texas. For a long time, Fulton was considered the head of navigation on the Red River due to its location at the Great Bend, and its proximity to White Oak Shoals, a shallow river ford, just to its west. Fulton was even slated to be a station on the country's first transcontinental railroad, which Secretary of War Jefferson Davis (who later became the President of the Confederacy, 1860-1865) advocated for in 1856.

42.*Fulton at the Great Bend of the Red River was on track (pun intended) to be on the transcontinental railroad in the 1850s, as this map attests (LOC).*

After the Civil War, Fulton continued to dominate the area. The Cairo and Fulton Railroad came through town,

followed by the Bankhead Highway, one of the first named
and marked highways to crisscross the United States. Sadly,
it was the Interstate that led to the town's downfall.
Interstate 30 (Fort Worth to St. Louis) bypassed Fulton,
Washington, and the Bankhead Highway. The Interstate,
coupled with a number of devastating floods in the last
decades of the twentieth century left Fulton unable to
recover.

*43. The last remnant of downtown Fulton was demolished in 2015.*

*The sights:* Unfortunately, there aren't many ghostly sights in
Fulton any longer. The lone old commercial building, which
was in a bad disrepair for a long time, was finally razed in
2015. The Great Bend is not easy to access, either. The
highway bridge over the Red River allows for a view of
platforms that were used in the 1930s for levee work, and
erosion controls, put in place by the WPA, are still visible as
well. Some antebellum homes – small and tidy – can be seen
along many of the streets in this well laid-out town, where

the sidewalks on Little River Street hint at the infrastructure that used to bet here. A small well house, with a cozy mural of people retrieving water, is on the river side along north Little River Street. The cemetery at Fulton is just to the north of town along AR 355, but is not marked. The cemetery sits next to a private house with "no trespassing" signs, so take caution. All of its old tombstones are simply gone, and the entire place is very much overgrown. However, the sunken road of the old path to the cemetery — quite possibly, this is also the old Trammel Trace — is easily spotted among the brush.

**By the way: Bankhead Highway**

The Bankhead Highway, as US 67 was called when enthusiasts and state legislators designated it as an interstate pathway in 1916 when it reached from Washington, D.C. to San Diego, California. Though the numbered highway system has slightly altered the route, travelers can still enjoy this road in its entirety if they want to eschew the interstates. Remains of the original roadbed parallel the current one in many parts of the sixteen-mile journey from Texarkana to Fulton. Two concrete bridge spans, with date plates, are easily visible on the eastern side of the road just outside of Texarkana.

## Washington (Hempstead County)

*What's to see*: An entire state park of preserved buildings scattered throughout town; two gargantuan trees; two very interesting cemeteries; the sunken trace of the Southwest Trail; an archive; and an abandoned high school.

*How to get there*: From Fulton, follow Ozan Street/ AR 195 northeast for about 14 miles. The old high school and the building that houses the Southwestern Arkansas Regional Archives will be on the south side of the road. Just a bit further up the road is the courthouse, which is now the headquarters for the state park. To get to the city's cemetery, take US 278 north past the Baptist Church.

45.*The historic tavern at Washington before its restoration looked a bit lopsided (LOC).*

*Some history*:

Settlement in the area that became Washington was already recorded in 1818, when Elijah's Tavern served travelers on the Trammel Trace. When Fort Towson was constructed in the newly created Indian Territory further west, the trace was widened and marked to become a military and postal road. This widening created Washington as a permanent settlement in 1824 and was designated as the Hempstead County seat in 1826. Washington had an ideal location along

*46.During the Civil War, the 1836 courthouse at Washington served as the seat for Arkansas's Confederate government. Both courthouses in Washington, Hempstead County's former seat, sit along the Southwest Trail, a very old road that has become a holloway, or sunken road, due to centuries of wear.*

a high ridge line away from the flood plains of the Red River, and thus became the western-most county seat in Arkansas Territory. Men and women from northern as well as other southern states came to Washington to find their luck as planters, pioneers, and merchants to serve troops, officers, migrants, farmers, Caddos and Shawnees, and Choctaws leaving their homelands for Indian Territory. Quickly, Washington built itself into a sizeable and well-outfitted town at the cross roads of several trails.

While most white, Washingtonian men voted for Whigs and opposed secession, the Arkansas legislature nonetheless moved to Washington during the Civil War to protect its state archives from possible Union destruction after the surrender of Little Rock in 1863. After the war, Washington continued as the county seat. The town's freed people built their own settlement, centered around a Masonic Lodge, on the north side of the town. By the 1870s, the Cairo and Fulton Railroad threatened Washington's prominence — instead of linking to the old town, the investors began selling land plots to create the new city of Hope. Although Hempstead County had built a large, new courthouse at Washington in 1874, citizens and commerce flocked to Hope instead. In 1938, they voted Hope as the county's new seat, much to the chagrin of Washingtonians.

*47.Washington has a number of historic ties to its deep African American history, like this Masonic Lodge on its westside.*

During World War II, the federal government designated the land surrounding another old settlement —

Marlboro — for the Southwest Proving Grounds, which led
to the destruction of several old settlements. For a while, all
this proved to a be death knell for the town, as more and
more people left and more and more of the area's buildings
and infrastructure decayed. Luckily, its citizens saw
opportunity. A few of the homes slated for demolition were
moved to Washington. In 1958, members of the Community
Improvement Club of Hempstead County and the
Foundation for the Restoration of Pioneer Washington
joined forces to create a "colonial Williamsburg" style
attraction for southwestern Arkansas. This led to the
restoration and eventual designation of the Washington
State Historic Park in 1978, and now this little ghost town
has become a highly interesting, authentic attraction.

*The sights:* Travelers should devote several hours to explore
historic Washington. Both the antebellum courthouse (1836)
and the "new" courthouse (1874) can be toured. The post
office in the downtown strip is designated as the oldest in
Arkansas. At the 1836 courthouse stands one of the world's
largest catalpa trees and, across the street, stands the state's
(world's?) largest magnolia tree. Washington's Franklin
Street is a destination itself, as it is a "holloway" — a sunken
trace (now paved) that is the original road which linked the
city to Little Rock and beyond. The town is still, for the most
part, laid out as it was for generations. Several picturesque
church buildings line the streets; the former jail is on
Conway Street; the restored tavern, which once hosted Sam
Houston, is in situ at the junction of the military road (aka
Southwest Trail) and the Trammel Trace; and the two former

schools are in their original locations on the opposite sides of the town.

The plethora of young women's graves in the town's pioneer cemetery behind the 1914 schoolhouse bears testament to the incredibly hard life married women had to endure. When one speaks of pioneers in the South, it is imperative to note that this term includes African American people, most of whom were enslaved (upon statehood in 1836, Arkansas made it illegal for Free People of Color to live in the state). Along US 278 sits the one of the first Masonic Lodges founded by African Americans in the Reconstruction era. Inside the pioneer cemetery are graves of several of the African American women who belonged to the many civic organizations that developed after the war. Washington's current cemetery sits about a mile north of town off US 278 and has hundreds of burials. The African American portion is still segregated by a fence at the back of the property.

*48.While the newest building for the Lincoln School, founded in 1868 for African American students in Washington, still stands, no school building serves students in Washington anymore. Instead, they go to school in Hope.*

**By the way: The Southwest Trail and Trammel's Trace**

The road between Washington and Fulton (AR 195) has two names: the Southwest Trail and the Trammel Trace. The historic (contemporary, or proper) name for this portion of the road is the term, Trammel Trace. Named after its most ardent user, Nicholas Trammell (actual spelling) who also owned a tavern along the road, the trace had been a trading path for Native Americans centuries prior in order to reach the salt flats east of the Red River, as well as to travel to the hot springs along the Ouachita River. When Nicholas Trammell began using the trail in the early 1810s, he did so to trade with Indians in Texas as well as, according to many accounts, shunt stolen horses back and forth. In Washington, the trace met up with the St. Louis– Little Rock– Washington military and postal road, which is now called the Southwest Trail. The military/postal road in Washington continued westward towards Fort Towson in Indian Territory, leaving the route between Washington and Fulton to commercial enterprises only — which is why emigrants to Texas, such as Stephen F. Austin and Sam Houston, utilized the Trammel Trace once they left Washington. The route of the St. Louis, Iron Mountain, and Southern Railway (later, the Cairo and Fulton Railroad) approximates the Southwest Trail.

**Ozan (Hempstead County)**

*What's to see*: Several abandoned commercial buildings.
*How to get there*: From McGaskill, return to Washington, then drive north on US 278 for about 7 miles.

*49.Downtown Ozan*

*Some history*: Named after a lumber company, Ozan's original name was Mound Prairie. It had its beginnings in 1817, but didn't become incorporated until 1888, after the Arkansas and Louisiana Railroad laid tracks through town in 1884. The uptick in saw mill work and lumber shipping brought new people into Ozan, where business boomed with several stores, mills, and even cafes. Though the Kansas City Southern Railway still winds its way past town, it no longer stops in Ozan, and thus the town's fortunes have slowly declined.

*The sights*: Overgrown remains of commercial buildings can be seen at the bend of US 278 and CR 22. On Mulberry Street (also named N. Wilbur Jones Street), the former school building is visible.

### Columbus (Hempstead County)

*What's to see*: Ruins of a school.

*How to get there*: From Ozan, return to Washington. Go south on AR 195, then turn west onto CR 14. Follow the road until it becomes AR 73, which goes into Columbus. To get to the ruins, turn south on the cemetery road (marked).

*Some history*: Columbus is an old town founded in 1834 with the establishment of its post office. Plantation owners, enslaved people, and employed workers made up the majority of this community's citizens before the Civil War. After the war, the town grew in size and featured grocery stores, a cotton gin, a grist mill, a hotel, and several churches. By the 1930s, a substantial school served the white students. Within a decade, however, school districts consolidated due to population losses. Columbus still had a number of stores up until the 1980s, but they have since shuttered, too.

*The sights*: Two giant archways are all that remain of the town's bricked school building, which loom above the town's well-kept cemetery.

### Okay (Howard County)

*What's to see*: Remains of a cement city.

*How to get there*: From Columbus, go west on AR 73 to Saratoga. Then, turn north on AR 355. Okay Road will be the first road on the left about two miles north of Saratoga. Follow Okay Road until it ends.

*Some history*: In the 1920s, the Ideal Cement Company from Denver, Colorado came into Howard County, Arkansas, found a huge deposit of limestone, and started a subsidiary branch of its Portland cement manufacture. The brand name of the cement was "OK" — not in the terms that it was awesome, but rather that it was part of the brand located in Ada, Oklahoma. The town that grew up around this company became known as Okay. The entire town was built with cement (go figure!) and sat on the southeastern side of Millwood Lake. It kept on making cement until the 1980s, when the plant closed.

*The sights*: Today, Okay is a true ghost town - the site is leased by a hunting and fishing club and is fenced off. Visitors can still glimpse part of the town all the way to the fence as well as with its church. Flyovers from Google Maps help a lot in making out the foundations of where the town used to be. After all, it's hard to erase traces of a building material that is meant to last.

**Not a Ghost but Almost: Tollette (Howard County)**

Tollette is north of Okay and Saratoga on AR 355. It was founded in the early 1870s by freed people from the surrounding communities as a stop for the Graysonia, Nashville, and Ashdown Railroad. Named after a Virginia man who helped to organize the town, Tollette grew into a sizeable community with stores, gins, a post office, grist mill, and, importantly, a doctor's office. In 1927, Tollette's early school was replaced by a more modern building partially funded by the Rosenwald Foundation, a philanthropic endeavor instituted by the Rosenwald family of Chicago to bring equity to segregated schools. The school expanded into the Howard County Training School, where animal husbandry, agriculture, and domestic arts were taught. Sadly, the school closed in 1972, and today, students in Tollette have to travel to the consolidated schools that serve rural Howard County. Now, the old school houses the town hall and library.

## Ben Lomond (Sevier County)

*What's to see*: Some abandoned commercial buildings.

*How to get there:* From Okay, go north on AR 355 back to Tollette. In Tollete, turn west onto AR 23/ Bright Star Road. This road will become Woodside Road. Follow the road west until it ends at the intersection with Main Street. Turn north on Main Street and follow it into "downtown" Ben Lomond.

*Some history*: While town names are often tributes to individuals, this is not the case with Ben Lomand. The tiny town was named after a mountain in Scotland, because the town's first settlers were from there. Ben Lomand, which was founded after the Civil War, thrived only briefly. Ever since its beginning, its population has been declining steadily.

*The sights*: Ben Lomond has a few commercial buildings left. The old gas station no longer sells gas, and the former mercantile no longer sells merchandise. A building from the former school has been turned into a community center.

## By the way: Old US 71

North of Wilton is the original road bed of US 71, one of Arkansas's first macadamized (paved) roads. Still sporting its original, sturdy surface, it's a nice little respite from the faster pace on the modern highway. To get to the best and most drivable remnant of old US 71, turn south onto a little road, called "Ashley Camp" on maps, prior to AR 234 meeting the new US 71/US 59. The road turns from dirt to pavement, and a series of bridges goes to a camp ground. There is no longer a bridge over the Little River, as the dam at Millwood Lake has backed up the river.

One of my more interesting "ghost town" encounters happened on the old US 71. I saw a seven-foot alligator sunning itself on the opposite side of a bayou next to the old road bed. I got out of my car to take a photo, but made too much noise, so the animal slid into the water. As I was looking for a way to climb back up the embankment, I heard water splashing behind me. I turned around and saw the alligator coming right towards me. I never climbed a hill that fast in my life.

### Wilton (Little River County)

*What's to see*: Remains of two grocery stores and a very rare railroad depot.

*How to get there*: From Ben Lomand, go south, then west, on Main Street/ AR 234 and follow it until it ends at US 59/ US 71. Turn south on US 59/US 71 to get to Wilton. The points of interest in Wilton are at the intersection of US 71/US 59/ Main Street and Texarkana Avenue.

51.A rare depot has been preserved in Wilton, Little River County.

*Some history*: As far as ghost towns go, Wilton is still fairly large, but it's slowly declining. A railroad town that was renamed in 1892 to honor a railroad executive, Wilton featured several businesses by the turn of the century, including fabrication businesses, and two public schools. However, even with the town's prominent location on the first paved highway in southwestern Arkansas, Wilton's schools were closed before WWII, and within thirty years, so were most of its businesses.

*The sights*: The impressive hulk of the S.S. P. Mills and Son mercantile, built in 1912, once sat at the intersection of US 71 and Texarkana Avenue but it has since been razed. Across from the ruin is a small cabin, which housed Wilton's first store. Between the store ruin and the train tracks on Texarkana Avenue sits the last remaining depot of the Texarkana and Fort Smith Railway. The depot was moved to its current location within the last twenty years.

### Alleene (Little River County)

*What's to see*: A log cabin that became a courthouse.

*How to get there*: Just north of downtown Wilton is AR 234. Turn west on AR 234 and follow it to a cardinal intersection. Here, AR 234 goes north; follow AR 234 north into Alleene.

*Some history*: Little Alleene never was much of a town, but in 1867, it became the first county seat of Little River County. Because of its location close to the geographic center of the newly formed county, the Arkansas legislature deemed William Freeman's front yard the first courthouse and jail. That's one way to enter politics.

Alleene was not the seat for very long – Little River County saw fierce competition in the quest for governmental dominance. The second seat, designated in 1868, became Rocky Comfort. But when the railroad bypassed Rocky Comfort, the town of Richmond erected a courthouse from its own coffers to lure the railroad. Railroads are fickle entities, however. Instead, the railroad came through Ashdown. Ashdown is currently Little River's county seat, but who knows, it might change.

*The sights*: The log cabin courthouse and jail are still present and can be visited.

### Winthrop (Little River County)

*What's to see*: A few commercial buildings, an old school that's been turned into a museum, and a calaboose.

*How to get there*: From Alleene, follow AR 234 northwest to Winthrop.

*52.Criminal history is on display in Winthrop, Little River County.*

*Some history*: Winthrop began life in the early twentieth century as a logging and farming community. Never a big town, it nonetheless invested in itself with a commercial strip, several lumber mills, cotton gins, a bank, a physician's office, a library, a large school, and even a one-room jail, also called a calaboose. In the 1960s, Winthrop Rockefeller, scion of the famed Rockefeller family from New York, launched his campaigns for governor due the coincidence in names. Why not?

*The sights*: Winthrop is still quite a lively place but is still a ghost town because its schools and most of its commercial district are derelict. Its old high school is now a museum, and the town's former jail sits, interestingly enough, behind the Baptist Church at Chestnut and Broad Streets.

This is the end of Arkansas's Red River Valley Ghost Town Tour!

Oklahoma's ghost town tour begins at Ultima Thule, which originally was an Arkansas border crossing. To get to Ultima Thule from Winthrop, go west on AR 234 to AR 41. Travel north on AR 41 to DeQueen. In DeQueen, turn west onto US 70 and follow it to the straight line that separates Arkansas from Oklahoma – or, in history, separated Arkansas Territory from Indian Territory. This is Ultima Thule.

**By the way: Ultima Thule**

"Ultima Thule" means "a distant territory or destination." Considering the reason why this little town was founded, the name is apt, indeed. This hamlet was the end line for the Choctaws and Chickasaws as they traveled from their original homelands to the unknown Indian Territory. Lying on an old military road (today's US 70) west of DeQueen, the non-descript border crossing served the tribes as the beginning of their lives in this new country. The original Ultima Thule sat on the Arkansas side, but the Choctaw Nation survey of 1834 placed it in Indian Territory. Today, the site of Ultima Thule is commemorated as a simple name of the first road inside Oklahoma that connects to US 70.

Ultima Thule serves as a reminder that the Red River Valley in Arkansas is full of towns that were once bustling, but are now no longer on maps at all. Towns like Richmond and Laynesport (Little River County), Paraclifta (Sevier County) and La Grange (Lafayette County) were considered pretty important in the antebellum period, but the post-war world was not kind to them. Laynesport, a river boat town, lost its population to other settlements as the railroads took hold. Richmond tried to keep its status as the seat of Little River County, but lost due to the arrival of the railroad in Ashdown. La Grange was once the county seat of Lafayette County, but a flashflood wiped it out. Another former county seat is Paraclifta, which lost to Lockesburg's more centralized location once Sevier County was carved into smaller portions in the mid-nineteenth century. By just studying the lost settlements of southwestern Arkansas, it is easy to see how rapidly populations shifted and moved in and out of this sparsely-inhabited place.

# Oklahoma Ghost Towns

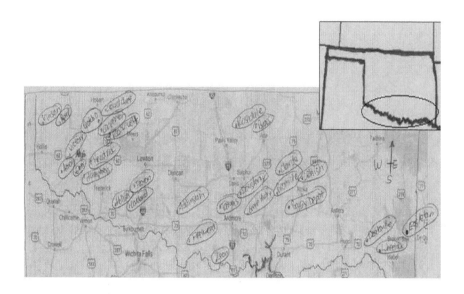

In Oklahoma, you'll begin your travel in the former Indian Territory and end in the former Oklahoma Territory, journeying from east to west. On the way, you'll pass through the Choctaw, Chickasaw, Comanche, Kiowa, and Apache nations. The tour covers: Eagletown, Wheelock Academy, Doaksville, Boggy Depot, Lehigh, Clarita, Bromide, Gene Autry, Dougherty, Byars, Rosedale, Tatums, Leon, Fleetwood, Addington, Faxon, Loveland, Hollister, Headrick, Elmer, Humphreys, Victory, Aaron School, Cooperton, Gotebo, Cloud Chief, Reed, and Vinson.

The recorded history of Oklahoma begins in 1824, when Indian Territory was created out of Arkansas Territory in preparation for the removal of native tribes who lived east of the Mississippi River. Southern states did not want to share their property with Indian tribes, even if the tribes had adopted many aspects of Anglo-Christian culture, including slave-holding. Thus, in the early 1820s, the states of Mississippi and Alabama negotiated treaties with Euro-Indian members of the Choctaw and Chickasaw tribes. The treaties promised that in exchange for giving up their homelands, the tribes would receive comparable land amounts in Indian Territory, plus monies from tribal land sales, all of which would be distributed and managed by Indian Agents of the Bureau of Indian Affairs. While several Choctaws moved very early to Indian Territory to avoid conflicts, the majority of both Choctaws and Chickasaws did not consider the treaties legitimate. They were rightfully suspicious that the signers received large, individual tracts of land separate from the communal properties that would be held by the rest of the tribe. The federal Indian Removal Act of 1830, condoned by President Andrew Jackson, supported the state–negotiated treaties, leading to forced removal under military escort.

Early settlements in the east of Oklahoma reflect a people who had to re-build their culture in a new land. Further west, towns developed alongside new industries, such as coal mining, tourism, railroad building, cattle driving, and ranching. Because of its history as a diaspora for southeastern tribes, many small Oklahoma towns have a real "frontier" feel to them — they are sparse, without cores, and feel temporary. For historians, these small settlements offer a contemporary look at the American past, as they reflect, in layout as well as temperament, the frontier towns established during the country's westward migration in the eighteenth and nineteenth centuries.

We'll commence our explorations at the entry point for the Choctaw and Chickasaw "Trail of Tears" and continue on a westerly path. If you decide to complete the entire itinerary, this tour will probably take you three or four days. Of course, you should suit yourself as to what you want to explore, and each segment of the tour can be taken in individual chunks.

### Eagletown (McCurtain County)

*What's to see*: A derelict downtown.

*How to get there*: Eagletown sits south of US 70 about ten miles west of the Arkansas border and about ten miles east of Broken Bow, Oklahoma. Turn south on Main Street and follow it to CR 4765 (the road across from the high school). Turn south on CR 4765 to get to the town's center.

54.*Downtown Eagletown, McCurtain County.*

*Some history*: Technically, Eagletown should not be considered a ghost town because it has a school. However, it's included because it has greatly diminished in size, in proportion to its significant historical importance. Or, to say it another way: since there really aren't any hard and fast definitions of ghost towns, it's alright to speculate.

Eagletown began as a small, predominantly Anglo-American settlement in the late 1810s, when the area was still a part of Arkansas Territory. However, the Anglos were forced off the land after several treaties were negotiated, which promised land in western Arkansas Territory to the Choctaws. The first one, signed by Andrew Jackson (at that point serving as an Indian Agent) and the Choctaws, created a reserve in Arkansas Territory. During James Monroe's administration, Indian Territory was carved out of Arkansas Territory in 1824. In 1828, the Indian Territory grew to the east by a sliver in the Eagletown area upon the correction of a survey error. Lastly, the Treaty of Dancing Rabbit Creek in 1830 provided both land and compensation for the Choctaws. All of these treaties brought waves of migrants.

*55.The Graham Grocery used to serve as Eagletown's post office (OHS).*

Eagletown (in Choctaw, Osi Tamaha) became the territory's first supply depot on the road between Washington, Hempstead County, Arkansas and Fort

Towson, Choctaw County, Oklahoma. The town grew, but only from temporary residents. Although the Choctaws who entered Indian Territory initially stayed in either Eagletown or down the road in Doaksville, many did so only briefly – they found better hunting in the mountains or better land for plantation building around the Red River. Thus, Eagletown's population fluctuated quite a bit. In the 1850s, the Choctaws carved counties within their nation, and Eagletown was designated the seat of the newly formed Eagle County. Eagletown's courthouse, post office, and supply depot hugged the military road, which approximates today's US 70. Even with its legal importance, the town remained small, though settlers who were not Choctaws began to populate the area by the late nineteenth century.

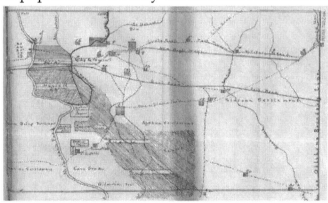

56.In 1932, Eagletown native Peter Hudson drew this map of Eagletown from memory for the Oklahoma Historical Society (OHS).

The Choctaw counties dissolved with subsequent treaties, which undermined their national autonomy. Eagletown came under McCurtain County — with the railroad town Idabel becoming the county seat — upon Oklahoma statehood in 1907. In 1910, the Texas, Oklahoma and Eastern Railroad constructed a line through the town to take advantage of the pine and cedar forests in the region. The Eagletown depot enticed businesses to build close by. Though the line was discontinued in the 1940s with the depletion of old growth timber, managed forestation has resurrected the industry in more modern times.

Before statehood, schooling in the Choctaw Nation generally relied on missionary schools. Eagletown's public school opened in the twentieth century, as the state's constitution mandated public schools. It still serves the sparsely-populated region.

*The sights*: Eagletown's downtown reflects both its railroad history and the loss of the settlement's importance as the railroad ceased operations in the 1940s. A few derelict store fronts can be seen just down the street from the well-maintained school buildings. On the west side of town along US 70 sits a simple church building that once served the faithful in Eagletown.

### By the way: Museum of the Red River

Along US 259 on the southern side of Idabel sits the world-renowned Museum of the Red River. This institution features artifacts from the Caddos, Choctaws, and other native people who, over the centuries, have called this area of the world home.

### By the way: Wheelock Academy

Along US 70 west of Idabel sits the 1832 Wheelock Academy, one of the oldest and best-preserved Indian schools in Oklahoma. And, of all of the missionary schools established by the Choctaws, Chickasaws, and several

protestant Christian denominations, Wheelock Academy is
the most historically intact. Named after the founder of
Dartmouth College, the Choctaw Nation and the Presbytery
dedicated the school as an all-girls academy, mainly due to
the influence of Choctaw preacher, Israel Folsom, who
advocated for the education of women. Wheelock was the
first Indian academy established west of the Mississippi
river, continuing a tradition of missionary academies that
had begun in the tribes' native homelands at the turn of the
nineteenth century. Students partook in science, math,
history, arts, and literature classes as well as religious and
labor instruction, but they were forbidden to speak their
language as the goal of the academy was to "Americanize"
the students. Constructed by both volunteer and enslaved

*57.The 1846 Presbyterian Church at Wheelock is the state's oldest stone church.*

labor, the complex had at one point sixteen buildings, and
often served as an inn for travelers and migrants. While it
closed down during the Civil War and suffered through a
fire, the academy re-opened in the 1880s and remained in
operation until the 1950s — in the latter years, Wheelock
acted as an orphanage and boarding school. In 1965, the

remaining buildings of the academy as well as the 1845 stone church, the earliest building of its kind in the Indian Territory, were designated a national historic landmark. Wheelock is now owned and managed by the Choctaw Nation. A cemetery surrounding the old church lists many "unknown soul" tombstones, as a cholera outbreak in the 1830s led to quick burials and shoddy record keeping.

### Doaksville (Choctaw County)

*What's to see*: Stone foundations and archeological artifacts. *How to get there*: From Eagletown, Idabel, or Wheelock Academy, continue west on US 70 until you get to Fort Towson. Travel through downtown Fort Towson to Red Road, on which you turn north and follow the signs to the cemetery. Turn into the cemetery and take the path all the way to the northeast corner, where you'll happen upon some stone stairs. These stone steps lead to a trail. Take the trail into the remains of Doaksville – some interpretive signs will help guide you.

*58.The former post office at Doaksville (OHS).*

*Some history*: Named after a storekeeper who traveled with the Choctaws from Mississippi in the 1820s, Doaksville gradually grew into the largest settlement within the Choctaw Nation. With a steamboat landing at the confluence of the Kiamichi and Red rivers, the town served as a supplier to the nearby fort, the Indian academies at Wheelock, Spencerville, Goodland, and Armstrong, and traveling migrants. Its existence also benefitted the nascent Anglo settlements in Texas like Pecan Point and Jonesboro (see page 175). The town's importance grew during the Civil War, when it became the capital of the Choctaw Nation from 1860 to 1863.

59.*Doaksville was made up of wooden buildings and brick chimneys (OHS).*

Most likely, Doaksville would be on maps today had not several events conspired to bring about its end. First, Fort Towson's decommission put a hurt on the town. Then, Doaksville lost its status as the capital. In 1902, the St. Louis and San Francisco Railway bypassed the town for a more southerly course. Doaksville's decline was rapid and complete — the old town got buried by dirt and overgrown by trees so much that resurrecting it required a concerted effort by archeologists. In the 1990s, the Oklahoma Historical Society, the Oklahoma Archeological Survey, and the University of Oklahoma did just that. The excavated remains, consisting of foundations, are what you will see when you visit this eerily forgotten town.

*The sights*: Interpretive signs explain the town's history and the ruins you'll see, which are numerous: the foundations of a jail, a tavern, a lodge, and a house are clearly identifiable. Communal wells are also scattered throughout the former settlement. As you traverse the area, make sure to take photographs only; it is a protected archeological site.

60.*The hotel ruin at Doaksville, a protected archeological site.*

### By the way: Fort Towson

On the east side of the town of Fort Towson is its actual namesake. Fort Towson served as one of the earliest forts in Indian Territory. Built in 1824, its purpose was to protect the Choctaws and Chickasaws from the Caddos, Quapaws, Osages, and Anglos, all who claimed the area as their own. Anglo-Americans who lived in Arkansas Territory and Mexican Texas were especially hostile to the fort, as they saw it as an enforcer of their own unjust removal from the area upon the creation of Indian Territory in 1824. The fort was burned down in a fit of Anglo rage, but was rebuilt and used as a staging area for the Mexican American War in 1846. Decommissioned by the federal government in the 1850s, the fort was resurrected briefly during the Civil by Texan and Choctaw confederates. After the war, the fort continued to decay, but its ruins are now a state historic site.

### By the way: The Lee and Jefferson Highways

Those who like to travel the old alignments of highways will find two preserved roads in Bryan County, Oklahoma. The old Lee Highway (US 70) can take travelers to Durant, and the old Jefferson Highway (US 69) leads travelers out of Durant. US 70 is part of the Robert E. Lee Highway, a National Auto Trails system road that connected Washington D.C. to San Francisco. Nationally, the Lee Highway is difficult to follow, because its route has been superseded by over a dozen other US highways and at least two interstates. In Oklahoma, the old route of the Lee Highway can still be followed, especially east of Durant. On the western side of Bokchito (east of Durant), simply turn south onto the Blue Highway/ Old 70 and follow the road into Durant, which becomes the city's Main Street. Caution: the road isn't in the best condition anymore, and can get tight around the bridges.

US 69 has been called the "Palm to Pine Road." It's better known as the Jefferson Highway, which extends from

New Orleans, Louisiana to Winnipeg, Manitoba, Canada. What's great about this old road is that most of it has not been taken over by other routes or interstates. From downtown Durant, go north on First Street/ OK 78, then turn northeast onto US Business 69/Armstrong Road. Continue going north/northeast through the towns of Armstrong and Caddo before meeting up again with the new, faster alignment of US 75/US 69. Caution: ruts and potholes make this a bumpy but vintage ride. Portions of original, tarred macadamized pavement are still present.

### Boggy Depot (Atoka County)

*What's to see*: A cemetery and a few level foundations.

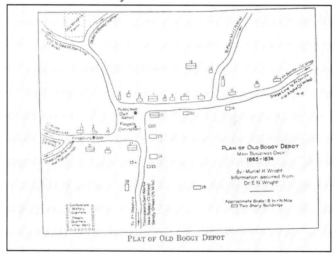

61. *The first official state historian, Muriel Wright, drew this map of Boggy Depot for the Oklahoma Historical Society. Wright's research remains a standard bearer for Oklahoma history. She is buried in the Boggy Depot cemetery.*

*How to get there*: From Fort Towson, go west on US 70 into Durant (or see the detour on the old alignment above; either path leads to Durant, the seat of Bryan County). In downtown Durant, turn north on 1st Avenue / OK 78. Continue north for 22 miles to Coleman. In Coleman, turn east onto Grand Street/ E 1890/ Overland trail/ West Boggy Depot Road and follow the road for about 10 miles into Boggy Depot State Park. Alternatively, drive north on US 75/ US 69 to Tushka, and turn west onto Boggy Depot Road to follow it to the park.

*Some history*: As the first seat of the Chickasaw Nation in Indian Territory, developed into one of antebellum Oklahoma's most important towns. From the 1830s to the 1840s the Chickasaws, many of whom were slave owners, leased the western part of the Choctaw Nation instead of immediately establishing their own nation. Apparently, prominent families were holding out for better land prices in the sale of their ancestral lands in Mississippi. They chose to build Boggy Depot as their center because its location was more than fortuitous — it was ideal. The town was laid out at the intersection of several important roads, including military traces, the Texas/Shawnee trail, the Gold Rush Road, and stage coach routes. Access to these trade venues opened up business opportunities, and Boggy Depot sported mills, gins, a bois d'arc seed factory, and a salt works. It was also a major trading center for Chickasaw plantations and ranches. In 1855, the Chickasaws officially established their new nation in Indian Territory. The new survey did not include Boggy Depot, however, as the established boundary lay just to the town's west. The Chickasaw nation's capital was moved about twenty miles west to the new town of Tishomingo.

During the Civil War, Union troops camped around Boggy Depot and engaged the Confederates, who were also encamped there. Historians are unsure of the exact location of the "skirmish at Middle Boggy Depot" but know that forty-seven men died in this timeframe, both in battle and from a measles epidemic. After the war, Boggy Depot continued as an important trading center, until the Missouri-Kansas- Texas Railroad, which was the first railroad built through Indian Territory, bypassed it by a good ten miles in 1872. Several residents moved to nearby Atoka and Tushka instead, and even founded New Boggy Depot along the railroad (this settlement was not successful). Because the railroad diminished the need for stage coaches, and cattle driving took place further to the west, Boggy Depot was pretty much gone by the turn of the twentieth century.

*The sights*: There's not much to see in Boggy Depot. Small signs point out where buildings used to stand — you'll see their stone outlines embedded in the ground, if you walk around long enough — and large, interpretive signs explain important points. Beyond the barbed wire fence in the southeastern portion of the old town, the roadbed that served the Butterfield Overland Main and Stagecoach (which traveled from St. Louis, Missouri to San Diego, California) is fairly easy to discern. At the northern end of Park Road lies Boggy Depot's large and impressive cemetery. The tombstones, many broken or illegible, make for great photographs. But, beware… something ghostly could happen to you here.

During one of my many visits to Boggy Depot, I wanted to photograph two identical tombstones that stood next to each other. As I stepped between the markers, I suddenly noticed the distinct scent of perfume. I looked around to see if fresh flowers had been laid somewhere in the cemetery, but I didn't see any. It was also very early in the Spring, and the wildflowers had not started blooming yet. Though I couldn't explain the smell, I simply shrugged off the phenomenon and raised my digital camera to take a picture. Instead of the cemetery, however, the camera's display only showed snow, with vertical lines moving through the screen in intervals. My camera had never done that before... so I decided to turn it off and then turn it back on, to see if the malfunction would cease — and the camera refused to power down. It dawned on me that I might be experiencing some kind of "event." I apologized for disturbing the graves, and slowly walked away from the cemetery to my car, never turning my back on the graveyard. Your mileage may vary on the weirdness factor of Boggy Depot's cemetery, of course, but come prepared with an open mind (and steely nerves), anyway!

## By the way: The Butterfield Overland Mail and Stagecoach Company

Just north of Boggy Depot on US 69 sits the Atoka Museum. The interior is dedicated to area history and is not very large, but the museum has an impressive collection outside. For one, it has a Confederate cemetery ... and it also sports some of the ruts of the Butterfield Overland Mail and Stagecoach route. Established in 1857, the Butterfield ferried passengers and mail between St. Louis, Missouri and San Diego, California as the first southern transcontinental stage coach. The Butterfield, founded by one of the original partners of the American Express stagecoach company, made its money not from passengers, but from delivering the mail. Upon secession of Arkansas and Texas in 1861, the legendary stagecoach closed in 1861 — after all, the U.S. mail would not run through enemy territory.

### Lehigh (Coal County)

*What's to see*: A closed bank and several abandoned gas stations.

*How to get there*: From Boggy Depot, go east on Boggy Depot Road to US 69/ US 75, then go north through Atoka. Follow US 75 to the west at the junction north of Atoka, and continue on US 75 to Lehigh.

*62.Commercial archeology in Lehigh, Coal County.*

*Some history*: Lehigh got its start in the 1880s as a coal mining town – that's why its name is Lehigh, which recalls a coal mining valley in Pennsylvania. The coal mines supplied fuel to at least three railroads, which crossed the burgeoning town by the beginning of the twentieth century. Several thousand people came into Lehigh to take advantage of the available work. However, laboring in coal mines is difficult, and low wages coupled with dangerous conditions and fatal mining disasters led miners to strike and unionize. This didn't sit too well with the railroad companies. They switched their locomotive technology to oil, leaving the coal mining industry in Coal County to dwindle. By the 1960s, Lehigh had lost its school, depot, and its bank. Although the town sits on a fairly busy highway and it still is home to farmers and residents, Lehigh is, commercially, a ghost.

*The sights*: You'll find several old gas stations on US 75, which used to be known as either the "Gulf Coast Highway" or "King of Trails Highway." Turn west on Main Street to visit the sturdy bank building, which is the only remnant of the once-thriving downtown Lehigh.

### Clarita (Coal County)

*What's to see*: A railroad bridge and some old-order Amish farmsteads.

*How to get there*: From Lehigh, go north on US 75 to Coalgate, then take OK 31 southwest for about 20 miles to its end at OK 48. Turn south on OK 48. Follow OK 48 for about 2 miles until you get to the first western turn-off, which is CR E1740. Turn onto CR E1740, then turn south on CR N3795/ Main Street and follow it into Clarita.

*Some history*: Clarita was a small farming community that built up around the Kansas, Oklahoma and Gulf Railway (later renamed the Missouri, Oklahoma and Gulf Railway) in the early twentieth century. Then, the railroad stopped coming through, and Clarita would have been nothing more than a spot on a map had the Old Order Amish not realized, in the 1970s, that it would be the perfect community to practice their faith and farming methods - though they use tractors because the Oklahoma soil is not the easiest to plow. *The sights*: Not much to see in Clarita, but it does have an Amish bakery that is occasionally open. South of Clarita on CR N3690/ Limestone Road (this is the road you will take to get to your next destination) is an abandoned but scenic railroad bridge that towers over the road and Walnut Branch Creek.

### Bromide (Coal County)

*What's to see*: A few disused, downtown buildings and several reminders of this former resort town.

*63.Bromide's first hotel (OHS).*

*How to get there*: From Clarita, follow CR N3795/ Main Street to CR E1750. Turn west on CR E1750 and then turn south on CR N3690/ Limestone Road. Past the railroad bridge is CR E1790/ Bromide Road. Turn west on CR E1790/ Bromide Road and follow it into town.

*Some history:* Bromide, originally known as Juanita as well as Zenobia, was built at the turn of the twentieth century when businessmen speculated that its mineral-rich waters might entice tourists to visit for spa vacations. Using stones quarried from the rocky hills on Bromide's north side, hotels and a swimming pool were soon constructed to

*64.A farmers' union meeting in Bromide in the 1920s (OHS).*

accommodate visitors, which during the spring and summer seasons could amount to over 10,000 people. To get to Bromide, the Kansas, Oklahoma and Gulf Railway (later, the Missouri, Oklahoma and Gulf Railway) built a spur into town to haul rock and, once a week, passengers. Bromide's prosperity only lasted about twenty years. Modern resorts situated on major highways — like Sulphur, Oklahoma and Mineral Wells, Texas — siphoned visitors away from Bromide. When the railroad stopped running in the 1950s, the town diminished even further.

*The sights:* The hulks of a few stone buildings sit along Bromide Road, and the word "Bromide" is spelled out in rock on a nearby hill. Several broken remains – including capped wells, the pool and the springs – sit on Main Street, but most of the historic evidence is on private property and is inaccessible.

## By the way: Wapanucka Academy

As you drive on Bromide Road, you'll pass Academy Road. Along Academy Road (southbound) stood the Wapanucka Academy, a Chickasaw boarding school for girls that opened in 1852. Its impressive stone buildings earned it the nickname, Rock Academy. During the Civil War, Confederates turned the building into a hospital; after the war, it once again served as a school until it was closed permanently in 1911. The stone building fell into ruin, and now only the foundation remains.

*65.The beautiful Rock Academy no longer stands (OHS).*

## By the way: Fort Washita

South of Tishomingo lie the ruins of historic Fort Washita, built in the 1840s to protect the Chickasaws from hostile area tribes. Constructed of native stone, the fort also served as a staging area for troops preparing for the Mexican-American War in 1846 and was a way station for dragoon expeditions, survey parties, and stage coach routes, including the famous Butterfield Overland line. Fort Washita was occupied by Confederate troops during the Civil War, who burned the complex. After the war, the Chickasaw Nation took over the fort and allotted the land to several tribal families, who also witnessed fires throughout the years. Luckily, the fort became a national register property in the 1960s. It is now a scenic park and museum. The clear indentation of the Old Military Road that snakes through the grounds is reason enough to visit this important place. To get to Fort Washita from Tishomingo, go south on US 377 to Madill. In Madill, drive east on OK 199 to get to the fort.

*66.Fort Washita is extremely scenic.*

### Gene Autry (Carter County)

*What's to see*: A small downtown that's seen better days, plus an old school building that hosts a museum.

*How to get there*: From Bromide, go south on OK 7D for two miles to OK 7. Turn west on OK 7 and drive to US 377/ OK 99, then head south on US 377/ OK 99 into Tishomingo. In

Tishomingo, drive west on OK 22 to Ravia, where you will continue driving west/southwest on OK 1 until it ends at US 177/OK 199. Turn west onto US 177/OK 199 and drive to Dickson. In Dickson, drive north on US 177 for about 25 miles. You will come to OK 53 — turn west here. Then, turn south on OK 53 A (close to the Ardmore Municipal Airport) to find Gene Autry.

*Some history*: Gene Autry was once known as Berwyn until the town changed its name in 1941 to honor the famous cowboy singer whose local ranch headquartered his traveling rodeo. Alas, the well-known name did not save this little town from its ghostly doom. Berwyn a.k.a. Gene Autry began life in the 1870s as a farming community. It had gins, a mill, stores, a grain elevator, a railroad stop (Gulf, Colorado and Santa Fe Railway) and a nearby air force base, but even with all of this activity, the town saw its population steadily decline after World War II. Luckily, the town knows how to live it up, even without too many actual lives living here. Citizens host a yearly music and film festival and also a jamboree – all named after Gene Autry, of course.

*The sights*: You'll find a few old commercial buildings by the still-active tracks. The Gene Autry Museum is inside the old high school on Grant Avenue.

### Dougherty (Murray County)

*What's to see*: An abandoned school and other remains.

*How to get there*: Getting to Dougherty, which sits nestled in the Arbuckle Mountains on the Washita River away from any major roads, is in no way a straight shot. From Gene Autry, go west on OK 53 to Springer. In Springer, turn north on US 77 and follow it through the Arbuckle Mountains. You will pass under Interstate 35 just north of Springer, and then you will pass over Interstate 35 north of Turner Falls Park. Just beyond the overpass at Interstate 35, turn southeast onto OK 110/ Kay Starr Trail (paved and dirt road). Continue following Kay Starr Trail for about ten miles – there are a few twists and turns, but nothing scary; the road is quite broad- until you reach Dougherty.

*67.Dougherty's depot now resides closer to Sulphur, Oklahoma (OHS).*

*Some history*: Dougherty actually still has a town government, but it is nowhere near the kind of city that it once was — especially since its school closed and students have to be bused to nearby Sulphur or Davis. Once known as either Henderson and Strawberry Flat, Dougherty was permanently renamed after a banker in the late 1880s whose investments enticed the Gulf, Colorado and Santa Fe Railway to erect a depot. The town grew into a sizeable settlement with the help of gravel, sand, and asphalt rock mining. It was considered to be a rough place, with several saloons and lots of fights. Nearby, a "burning mountain" — thought to have begun burning by lightning that struck either a natural gas or tar seam — brought considerable tourist attention. When the depot closed, however, much of the town's population moved away. There are still about 200 people that call Dougherty home. Trains, including the Amtrak passenger train *Heartland Flyer*, still pass through the town, though they no longer stop.

*The sights*: Downtown Dougherty is pretty much abandoned save for a gas station. The school, which sits on North 2nd Street, is very pretty. The concrete platform that was once part of Dougherty's depot sits along the tracks. Several hollow shells of buildings hint at Dougherty's former importance, including a large sand mining complex on Chickasaw Street (best accessible in late fall, winter, or early spring). Dougherty's depot can now be seen sitting on the side of OK 7 on the west side of Sulphur. It was converted into a restaurant, though as of this writing, it was no longer in operation.

### By the way: Turner Falls

As you drive north on US 77 (which was called the "Hobby Highway" back when it was a National Auto Trail), you will be rewarded with beautiful vistas of the Arbuckle Mountains, including a panoramic view of Turner Falls, the seventy-foot tall waterfall along Honey Creek. The falls lie in Turner Falls Park, an old tourist spot now managed by the city of Davis. The park offers natural pools and creeks, hiking trails, camping sites, shopping opportunities for original art inside vintage trading posts, and a chance to visit the ruins of a "castle" built on the side of a hill by an eccentric professor.

## Not a Ghost but Almost: Byars (McClain County)

*What's to see*: Downtown buildings and a really cool railroad bridge.

*How to get there*: From Dougherty, follow OK 110/ Kay Starr Trail northeast all the way to the east side of Davis. Then, turn east on OK 7 and travel to Sulphur. In Sulphur, drive north on US 177 past Stratford, then turn west on OK 59 and follow it to Byars.

*68.Downtown Byars in the 1940s, when it was a bit busier (OHS).*

*Some history*: In the early twentieth century, two railroads converged just below the small settlement of Johnsonville. Byars was born when the tracks of the Atchison, Topeka and Santa Fe Railway met the Oklahoma Central Railway. This made Johnsonville a ghost town, but Byars itself is gradually coming to the same status. Once the trains stopped coming through, the town began shedding population. Luckily, it still has an elementary school, but the rest of its students graduate high school in other nearby communities.

*The sights*: The buildings surrounding the square in downtown Byars are pretty banged up, though a small store and a plumber (as of this writing) still operate downtown. Go north on 2$^{nd}$ Street/ Johnsonville Avenue to see remains of the Oklahoma Central Railway and what might be a stone remnant of old Camp Arbuckle, which was built in the 1850s as a gathering point for travelers bound for the California gold rush who needed military escorts to accompany them through Comanche, Cheyenne, Arapaho, and Kiowa territories. The old Johnsonville cemetery is worth a visit, too. Continue north on the Railroad Bridge Drive to cross the Canadian River atop the re-purposed railroad truss bridge. Because the roadbed on the bridge allows only one car at a time to pass, ensure to watch for oncoming traffic.

**By the way: Old Platt National Park**

Sulphur is the gateway to the Chickasaw National Recreation Center, Oklahoma's only national park. Since the sulfur springs that emerged from the nearby mountains seemed to have restorative qualities, local ranchers created resorts and conference centers in the late nineteenth century. It was not just the water that made this land eligible for national protection, though — the Travertine and Rock Creeks are part of an important transition environment between the Gulf Coastal plains and the Cross Timbers prairies. When the Chickasaws deeded several hundred acres to the United States to create a national park in 1906, the original town of Sulphur Springs was moved to its new location. Technically, that makes the Chickasaw National Recreation Center also, in a small way, a ghost town, and the national park was originally called the Platt Historic District for this reason (named after Orville Platt, a Connecticut Senator who championed the park). The recreation area offers hiking, biking, camping, and swimming opportunities. Within the park, you can visit the original and very smelly sulfur water fountain, as well as some of the old town's roads. The Civilian Conservation Corps of the 1930s went on a building craze throughout the park and evidence of their craftsmanship abounds.

### Rosedale (McClain County)

*What's to see*: The remains of downtown.

*How to get there*: From Byars, drive west on OK 59 for about 15 miles to Rosedale.

69.*What's left of downtown Rosedale, McClain County.*

*Some history*: From the onset, Rosedale existed as an agricultural settlement and remained one, even when the Oklahoma Central Railway entered town in the early twentieth century. Although not one of the "black towns" platted specifically for African Americans (see the next entry on Tatums for more information about Oklahoma's "black towns"), many farmers who called Rosedale home were Chickasaw freedmen who received land allotments. The settlement declined with the cessation of rail traffic, the closing of the school, and an overall decline in farming. *The sights*: A little, bricked store front and a lone bank vault, sitting atop of a high-curbed sidewalk, constitute the remains of downtown Rosedale.

### Tatums (Carter County)

*What's to see*: Some nice buildings and a lot of history. *How to get there*: From Rosedale, drive west on OK 59 to OK 74. Turn south on OK 74 and follow it for about 40 miles. Lastly, turn west on OK 7. The first town you'll enter is Tatums.

*70.Tatums was home to the first oil refinery owned by African Americans (OHS).*

*Some history*: After the Civil War, all people who were enslaved were freed — this included the people held in bondage by the Chickasaws and Choctaws. According to their post-Civil War treaties with the federal government, both tribes were required to distribute land to the freedmen in their respective nations. The land was allotted in clusters, with African Americans establishing their own independent communities as a safeguard against racism. Rosedale (see above) can be considered an example of this kind of community. The other kind of all-black community developed after the Oklahoma Land Rush, when tribal land became available to all homesteaders. African Americans fled the Jim Crow south in hopes of establishing their own businesses, farms, and independence on the Oklahoma prairies — newspapers called them "Exodusters." Tatums exemplifies this latter kind of settlement. It started when the Tatums family, who ran a small store, applied for a post office. Soon, several people moved to the little community, and it developed into a town with a gin, mill, hotel, and gas stations. Tatums was also home to the nation's first oil

*71. Varner's Grocery also once served as Tatums' post office.*

refinery owned by African American businessmen. Citizens built their community's school in part with funds acquired through the Julius Rosenwald Foundation, which matched their own monetary and in-kind contributions. Julius Rosenwald was an executive at Sears, Roebuck and Company as well as a philanthropist who helped fund the

building of black schools in the segregated South. The
Rosenwald Fund assisted many, if not most, rural, black
schools in the Red River Valley. Sadly, several of these all-
black towns no longer exist in any physical form, and those
that do are the worse for wear as they have become historic
relics of the desegregation orders after 1954. Tatums is like
that — though people still live in here, it is no longer
commercially viable.

*72.Church services still commence in Tatums on Sundays.*

*The sights*: The old Rosenwald school has been demolished,
unfortunately, but a newish school now acts as a community
center. A cement-block grocery store now sits forgotten on
Lincoln Street. Tatums' Baptist church, which is still well-
visited and also hosts a plaque explaining the town's history,
is a real show stopper in its grace and simplicity. Another
plaque describing Tatums' hotel sits across OK 7 in an
overgrown field. The town's cemetery has older as well as

newer graves, with hand-carved markers and tombstones decorated with very detailed artwork.

### Leon (Love County)

*What's to see*: A town that could stand a little TLC.

*How to get there*: From Tatums, drive southwest on OK 7, then turn south onto OK 76. Follow OK 76 southward through Healdton and Wilson until the road ends in Leon.

*Some history*: Leon was part of the Ike Cloud ranch, a large, antebellum cattle breeding operation that helped to steer Texas cattle drives into Indian Territory. When Cloud died, his heirs subdivided the ranch, and by the 1880s, a farming community calling itself Leon applied for a post office. A German doctor became a major civic promotor at the turn of the twentieth century, but it was for naught: the town kept dwindling in size due to the Great Depression and urban job growth that siphoned the young generation away from

Leon's rural location.

*The sights*: Leon's downtown has a few non-descript buildings. The cemetery is quite large and features interesting tombstones. Leon's empty school sits on the southern edge of town and looks a little like something out of a 1970's horror movie: industrial and graffiti-covered.

**Fleetwood (Jefferson County)**

*What's to see*: An old store.

*How to get there*: From Leon, return on OK 76 to OK 32. Follow OK 32 west to Ryan, then turn south onto US 81. At Terral, turn east on Main Street and follow the road for about five miles to Fleetwood. Make sure to keep your eyes peeled for the store, as it is quite overgrown, and there aren't any signs pointing you to it. The building is on the north side of the road.

*Some history*: When drovers bound for Abilene, Kansas entered Indian Territory at Red River Station (Montague County, Texas), some began their long trek north by visiting a small supply stop that was manned by Chickasaw traders. Fleetwood, named after the land's owner, built up around the store, and soon a cotton gin and school served the rural community. Additional travelers bound for Fort Sill kept the store in business, but then the Chicago, Rock Island and Pacific Railroad laid their tracks about five miles west of Fleetwood. Residents moved to Terral, the nearest stop, and Fleetwood died.

*The sights*: The store, a long brick building riddled with bullet holes, is the only remain of Fleetwood. A small marker in the brush in front of the store explains the town's history.

**By the way: San Bernardo**

Rounding the bend of the Red River at Petersburg is the closest one can get to the ancient site of San Bernardo. Although it is a Spanish name, the settlement was never under Spanish rule. Instead, it was a Wichita village in which Bernard de la Harpe may have set up a trading post in the early eighteenth century (see page 20 for more

information). The village extended to both sides of the Red
River. In the 1830s or 1840s, an American man named
Holland Coffee established another trading post at this
location, but had to leave it as he was not authorized to trade
in Indian Territory. He moved onto a land grant in Grayson
County, Texas where he founded the town of Preston (see
page 185).

### By the way: The Chisholm Trail

One of the most fabled trails in the United States is
the Chisholm Trail, a road that took longhorn cattle from
Texas to their doom in Abilene, Kansas from 1866 to the late
1870s. Though the trail was not in commission for very long,
it proved to be an economic juggernaut for Texas, Indian
Territory, and Kansas. The trail, which contemporaries
called "The McCoy Trail" or "The Abilene Trail," actually
existed only in Indian Territory and Kansas. Under the
business sense of Joseph McCoy, a cattle handling
entrepreneur, Tim Hersey and his crew surveyed the route
from Kansas to the area around today's city of Enid. South
thereof, the trail extended from a series of feeder trails that
linked to Texas feeder trails at the Red River. Along your
ghost town tour, the original path of this trail lies about a
mile east of US 81. The ghost towns of Fleetwood and
Addington, Oklahoma (see below) are also chronicled in
*Traveling History Up the Cattle Trails*. The moniker "Chisholm
Trail" may have derived from cowboys who recounted that
Jesse Chisholm owned a store at the Canadian River along
the route.

## Addington (Jefferson County)

*What's to see*: A downtown, a jail, and a monument.

*How to get there*: From Terral, drive north on US 81 past Ryan and Waurika to Addington.

*Some history*: Addington got its start as a railroad town along the Chicago, Rock Island and Pacific Railroad, which was strategically placed to mirror the Abilene, a.k.a., Chisholm Cattle Trail. Soon, people flocked from all over to call Addington home, as it had cotton gins, a brick plant, stockyards, a lumberyard, a bank, and a good school. But the Great Depression and later, war work, enticed residents to move to the bigger cities of like Altus and Lawton. The churches remain active and several people still call Addington home, but it's nowhere near what it once was.

74. *The bank that surrounded this vault in Addington is long gone.*

*The sights*: A strip of abandoned buildings along US 81 mark Addington's downtown. A vault, hidden behind overgrowth, is the only standing reminder of a bank that saw a series of bank robberies in the 1920s. Across from the bank is Addington's jail, freshly painted in red with a gabled roof. To see an authentic place of Chisholm Trail lore, go west on Monument Road (last road inside Addington as you travel north on US 81). About two miles down the road stands an impressive monument that commemorates the Chisholm Trail. The monument sits on a high hill, which served as a landmark and look-out point for cattle drives. You can find the grave of Tim Lattimore, an African American cowboy who wanted to be buried on the trail, on the west side of the monument area. From the hill, you will have a fantastic view of the surrounding landscape, plus you'll be able to discern depressions at the western base of the hill that indicates the original trail.

*75.The beautiful setting of the monument outside of Addington, Jefferson County.*

**By the way: The Meridian Highway**

As you drive on US 81, you will be traversing the Meridian Highway, one of the oldest north-south connectors in the United States. Running from Canada all the way to Mexico, the highway's name came from its location – it lies on top of the ninety-seventh longitude (from Greenwich). In Oklahoma, the highway's name reflects an additional layer of history. It parallels the ninety-eighth Meridian, which reflects several boundaries: the "Indian Meridian" by which all Oklahoma surveys are measured; the established boundary line between the Chickasaw Nation and the Kiowa-Comanche-Apache Reserve; and the separation of the southern Indian Territory from the newly established

*76.Scene along US 81 shows the Meridian Highway that parallels the Indian Meridian, that parallels the Chicago Rock Island Railroad, that parallels the cattle trail crossing.*

Oklahoma Territory. Lastly, the Meridian Highway also mirrored the famous words of historian Walter Prescott Webb, who argued that the ninety-eighth meridian marked the line "where the west begins." US 81 is Oklahoma's original "tourist road." Officially, it parallels the Chisholm Trail, with many markers and museums explaining the world-famous cattle road along the way.

### Faxon (Comanche County)

*What's to see*: A school, lots of abandoned buildings, and a truss bridge.

*How to get there*: From Addington, drive north to Comanche on US 81. Go west on OK 5/ OK 53 towards Walters. Continue about 25 miles west past Walters to turn north on OK 36. You will drive through Chattanooga and come to Faxon.

*77.Faxon is a nice ghost town but boy, is this building ugly.*

*Some history*: Faxon is another railroad town that grew substantially at the turn of the twentieth century, but then steadily declined until, by the turn of the 21st century, it counted less than a fifth of its former population. The infrastructure that remains suggests a much larger community, which included several newspapers, two cotton gins, clothing stores, and at least one hotel. When the Chicago, Rock Island and Pacific Railroad stopped coming through, Faxon stopped growing.

*The sights*: The substantial brick school house can be found on 8th Street; several lonely commercial buildings – including a large gas station/ hotel/ restaurant with wagon-wheel windows - sit on 7th street; and West Cache Creek can be crossed along the Old Highway (take A Street or SW Holiday Road south of OK 36).

### By the way: Lone Wolf v. Hitchcock (1903)

The road towards Faxon reveals Oklahoma's political history. Faxon lies inside the Kiowa-Comanche-Apache Reservation, which was officially designated as such in 1901. After the Red River Wars ended in 1875, the Kiowas, Comanches, and Apaches lived in and around communal lands at Fort Sill. However, the United States government wanted land to be held privately, not communally, and thus opened the lands to homesteading and railroading. First, each individual tribal member received a "reserved" tract of 160 acres (survey errors made that number considerably smaller, however). Then, the remaining acreage was to be allotted to pioneers via government lottery, or by land development companies that railroad corporations operated. Though the Kiowas fought against this land grab, the Supreme Court sided with Congress in the landmark case of *Lone Wolf v. Hitchcock* (1903), which stated that the United States had final control over Indian lands. This is why most settlements in the area west of the ninety-eighth meridian were founded by whites.

### Loveland (Tillman County)

*What's to see*: Not much, considering how busy it used to be.
*How to get there*: From Faxon, go southwest on OK 36 until you get to CR E1870 north of Grandfield. Turn west on CR E1870 and follow it into Loveland.
*Some history*: Loveland is a farming community that was founded along the Wichita Falls and Northwestern Railway in 1908. The original name of Harriston was rejected by the post office, so the odd but romantic name Loveland was selected instead (people used to send their Valentine Day cards through Loveland for the postmark). Three grain elevators, two cotton gins, a newspaper office, stores, and lumberyards made this town a center for farmers. Though the Wichita, Tillman and Jackson Railway still passes through town, it no longer stops. This, coupled with drought and population shifts, allowed Loveland to decline.
*The sights*: There's the base of a water tower at a crossroads and a bank vault in someone's front yard.

### Hollister (Tillman County)

*What's to see*: The remains of a school.
*How to get there*: Hollister is just up the road from Loveland. From Loveland, go north on CR N2355, then turn west on CR E1860. Then turn north on N2320, then again west on CR E1850 and follow it to OK 54. Hollister is just north of the intersection of CR E1850 and OK 54. Since the roads aren't marked in this section of the world, it's easier to follow this

rule of thumb: follow the broad road that has crushed, white rock as the base.

*78.What was once a substantial school in Hollister, Tillman County.*

*Some history*: Like Loveland, the town of Happy (later, Hollister) was founded when the Wichita Falls and Northwestern Railway came through in 1907. Several people moved to the town from nearby smaller communities. By the 1920s, Hollister had an impressive school building, cotton gins, stores, a bank, several churches, and even a city band. Hollister's population declined as the younger generation moved away to find work in larger cities, and it's now a shadow of what it once was.

*The sights:* An old gas station and several empty, concrete pads hint at what used to be. Along Wilburn Avenue, the impressive façade of the old school reminds one of a Greek ruin.

### Headrick (Jackson County)
*What's to see*: A wind-blown hotel and a fantastic pair of bridges.

*How to get there*: From Hollister, follow OK 54 north to OK 5. Turn west, then north on OK 5 to Tipton. In Tipton, keep following OK 5 west to US 283. Go north on US 283 to Altus, then turn east on US 62. Take the marked exit to Headrick, which sits on the original alignment of US 62.

*Some history*: Headrick was a planned town built along the Oklahoma City and Western Railroad, but most of its citizens came from nearby Navajoe. They actually moved many of their own buildings from Navajoe to the new townsite. Headrick grew into a sizeable farming community, but declined when it lost its school due to a location dispute. Then, US 62 was straightened out, cutting the community away from the highway, as travelers could bypass the businesses in the town in favor of nearby Altus.

79.*Former hotel along the Ozark Trail in Headrick, Jackson County.*

*The sights*: A two story hotel, which must have looked very pretty when it still sported paint, sits among high grass on Main Street. Drive on the old US (CR E1645) east of Headrick to visit two closed bridges. The first bridge is a pony truss over the North Fork of the Red River. The second bridge is a full steel truss that crosses over the still-active tracks of the Burlington Northern and Santa Fe Railroad. Cars are no longer allowed on the bridges, but they can be walked.

## By the way: The Ozark Trail

US 62 is part of the Ozark Trail, a series of private roads built by automobile owners in the early twentieth century. Marked by obelisks, tourists could follow the roads from St. Louis, Missouri to Santa Fe, New Mexico. Many of these early roads would be later incorporated into the federal and state highway systems. The Ozark Trail from St. Louis to Oklahoma City, and then from Amarillo to Tucumari, would be numbered as the famous US 66.

## Elmer (Jackson County)

*What's to see*: A sturdy old bank that is now the town's post office.

*How to get there*: From Headrick, go west on US 62 to Altus. In Altus, turn south on US 283. Close to the Texas border will be E1750/ Main Street. Turn west to get to Elmer (there are signs, too).

*Some history*: Elmer was once a prosperous farming town that profited from its location on the Kansas City Mexico and Orient Railway. In fact, the town's name stems from a railroad executive. Once the home of a hotel, cotton gins, and lumberyards, the Dust Bowl's long drought contributed to its demise.

*The sights*: The landscape around Elmer is very much agricultural — it's very evident that this is the southern edge of the Great Plains. Elmer itself is fairly neat, with a post office that once was a two-story, brick bank. Even the railroad took up its tracks. Dogs might follow you around as you scope out the sights.

### Humphreys (Jackson County)

*What's to see*: A large school building with no roof.

*How to get there*: From Elmer, return to US 283 and drive north. Turn east onto E1690. Turn south onto CR 209 just before the railroad tracks. Then, turn east onto the first dirt road, N. Broadway. Because there aren't any trees to obstruct the view, the abandoned school is easily seen from the road.

*80.Beautiful school ruin in Humphreys, Jackson County.*

*Some history*: Humphreys doesn't exist on maps anymore. It tried to be a town, and until the 1960s, it had a school and even a teacherages (cottages) to ensure that the schools were manned. While the community still produces cotton on a large scale, its population loss has left it a ghost town.

*The sights*: The school's impressive hulk is now a storage space for farmers in the community. I also found an old cannon in someone's yard — it may have been used to scare off birds.

### Victory (Jackson County)

*What's to see*: Remains of a once-busy intersection and foundations of the school.

*How to get there*: Return to US 281 from Humphreys and drive north to Altus. In Altus, turn west onto US 62 and drive six miles to a large cemetery. At the cemetery, turn north onto N1980 and follow the road into what's left of Victory.

*81.Lonely store building in Victory, Jackson County.*

*Some history*: Although the building is long gone, the town of Victory centered on its school. Several smaller, one room school houses consolidated into the Victory School (opened in 1912) in 1921. The Victory School became noted for its dedication to academics and rigor and earned the honor of being "one of the top performing schools in Oklahoma." The town of Victory began a bit earlier than that. In the 1890s, the

Altus, Wichita Falls and Hollis Railway placed a stop at a farming settlement that named itself Victory when it received a post office. The little town boasted gins, mills, gas stations, restaurants, a bank, and stores. The school, which suffered a fire and then was rebuilt, closed in 1956 due to population loss. For a short period, the school building served as a children's home, but it eventually closed, too. This, of course, meant that the community itself scattered in the wind.

*The sights*: The former school's foundations and founder's stone sit at the original site, which is still tended and cared for by locals. A couple of commercial buildings, open to the sky, as well as a grain silo can be seen along the road.

### By the way: Aaron School and a Cowboy's grave

South of Victory on E1670 sits a lone cowboy's grave near a ditch. This is the resting place of Joel Moseley, a cowboy who died in 1890 from a trail accident and was buried where he met his fate. County workers encased the grave in concrete and added a granite headstone to prevent further deterioration of the site. Further down the road is the old Aaron School, which is now derelict but used to be two stories tall.

### Not a Ghost but almost: Roosevelt (Kiowa County)

*What's to see*: Ruins of an entire town that still operates normally.

*How to get there*: Return to Altus. From there, go north on US 283. In Blair, head east on OK 19 to Roosevelt. Or, follow US 62 east to the intersection with US 183. Go north on US 183 into Roosevelt.

*Some history:* Roosevelt's namesake was President Theodore Roosevelt, who visited the area in 1903, two years after the town came into existence as a speculation scheme by the Parkerburg Development Company. The St. Louis and San Francisco Railway came through town shortly thereafter, and the town boomed with several banks, a bottling plant, nice hotels, a newspaper, millinery, a department store, restaurants, and well-appointed schools for both black and white children. The Great Depression, however, was not kind to Roosevelt. Sitting in the Dust Bowl spelled doom for much of its population. With the U.S. entry into World War II, the lure of bigger cities with military bases, such as Altus, Lawton, and Wichita Falls, siphoned even more residents. Eventually, the schools closed, the trains stopped picking up passengers, farms turned corporate, and the town's businesses closed. Today, the entire town is home to an automobile scrapping and salvaging operation that sends train loads of car parts overseas for recycling.

*82.Roosevelt's downtown had a well in the middle of the street (OHS).*

*What's to see*: Roosevelt is definitely not growing, but the activity in the town belies that. Its downtown is a real wonder: on both sides of US 183 sit abandoned and ruinous buildings, including two banks, a large high school, a department store, a lodge, and a hotel. The segregated school, built by the Works Progress Administration on the 1930s, sits at Wood and Hamilton streets. Its post-segregation elementary school at Dunn and Tiffany streets has been converted into a senior center. The town hall, housed in one of the bank buildings along Main Street, is open only sporadically. Weed-strewn lots punctuate the city. Residents have to drive to Hobart or Snyder to do their shopping. Still, Roosevelt's feed mill remains open, has a city hall, and trains still stop at the silos. The town has also become home to a massive automobile salvage operation. The entire south end of Roosevelt is inundated with junk cars that are being parted out and recycled. The whole time I visited, large trucks rumbled through town, carrying corn, cotton, and cars. It was surreal, to say the least.

*83. Today's downtown Roosevelt is relatively quiet, at least inside its buildings.*

## Cooperton (Kiowa County)

*What's to see*: Disused bank and commercial buildings, two abandoned churches, a former school, and distinctive architecture.

*How to get there*: From Roosevelt, turn east on OK 19 and follow the road as it makes a turn northward. Cooperton lies about a mile further north on OK 19 on the western side of the highway. The overgrown infrastructure of the town can still be spotted along the dirt roads off the highway.

*Some history*: Cooperton was founded in anticipation of the land run on the Kiowa-Comanche-Apache Reservation. Though land distribution was decided by lottery, the incorporator was able to secure the land anyway, and Cooperton became a town. The bank, the general store, and several commercial buildings in the little town sport "cannonball" architecture. Using the rounded stones found along the Washita River in the Wichita Mountains to build structures, this distinctive and indigenous architectural material is well represented in the ruins of Cooperton.

*What's to see*: The old bank is a pin-neat gem, as is the regal, abandoned wooden church a block south of the bank. The general store is overgrown but sturdy. Sidewalks hint at the town's former optimism. The ghost town's community center is located in the old school yard, next to its large gym. The old Baptist Church no longer greets parishioners but still has the outhouses for its ghosts to use.

### By the way: Wichita Mountains

To the east of Cooperton lies the Wichita Mountains Wildlife Refuge and Wilderness Area. A large herd of bison roams the scenic park. On the eastern side of the Wichita

Mountains is Mount Scott inside which, according to Kiowa legend, the remaining buffalo retreated after the Americans hunted them to near extinction. Old Lady Horse, a Kiowa medicine woman, told the legend of the "Last of the Buffalo:"

*Everything the Kiowas had came from the buffalo. Their tipis were made of buffalo hides, so were their clothes and moccasins. They ate buffalo meat. Their containers were made of hide, or of bladders or stomachs. The buffalo were the life of the Kiowas. Most of all, the buffalo was part of the Kiowa religion. A white buffalo calf must be sacrificed in the Sun Dance. The priests used parts of the buffalo to make their prayers when they healed people or when they sang to the powers above.*

*So, when the white men wanted to build railroads, or when they wanted to farm or raise cattle, the buffalo still protected the Kiowas. They tore up the railroad tracks and the gardens. They chased the cattle off the ranges. The buffalo loved their people as much as the Kiowas loved them. There was war between the buffalo and the white men. The white men built forts in the Kiowa country, and the woolly-headed buffalo soldiers shot the buffalo as fast as they could (...)*

*Then the white men hired hunters to do nothing but kill the buffalo. Up and down the plains those men ranged, shooting sometimes as many as a hundred buffalo a day. Behind them came the skinners with their wagons (...) Sometimes there would be a pile of bones as high as a man, stretching a mile along the railroad track. The buffalo saw that their day was over. They could protect their people no longer. Sadly, the last remnant of the great heard gathered in council, and decided what they would do.*

*The Kiowas were camped on the north side of Mount Scott, those of them who were still free to camp. One young woman got up very early in the morning. The dawn mist was still rising from Medicine Creek, and as she looked across the water, peering through the haze, she saw the last buffalo herd appear like a spirit dream. Straight to Mount Scott the leader of the herd walked. Behind him came the cows and their calves, and the few young males who had survived. As the woman watched, the face of the mountain opened. Inside Mount Scott the world was green and fresh, as it had been when she was a small girl. The rivers ran clear, not red. The wild plums were in blossom, chasing the red buds up the inside slopes. Into this world the beauty of the buffalo walked, never to be seen again.*

*Alice Marriott and Carol K. Rachlin, American Indian Mythology (New York: Thomas Y. Crowell, 1968), 169-70. Quoted in Our Hearts Fell to the Ground: Plains Indians Views on How the West was Lost, ed. by Colin G. Colloway (New York: Bedford/St. Martin's, 1996), 129-30.*

**Not a Ghost but Almost: Gotebo (Kiowa County)**

*What's to see*: An entire downtown, and a fairly new but desolate school.

*How to get there*: Head about 15 miles north of Cooperton on OK 54 to Gotebo.

*Some history*: Originally named Harrison, the town was founded in 1901 along the tracks of the Chicago, Rock Island and Pacific Railroad and renamed Gotebo in honor of a respected Kiowa chief. Gotebo quickly developed into a large town, with lodges, newspapers, department stores, drug stores, hotels, restaurants, mills, and gins. Until fairly recently, Gotebo was a thriving community, and it still retains its town hall and overall community spirit. But Gotebo began shrinking as many businesses folded, and citizens commuted to either Lawton or Altus for jobs. The downtown decayed, and families moving away forced the school to close in 1990. Gotebo is one of the Red River Valley's newest ghost towns.

*84Gotebo's first department store, Wedel's, opened in 1909.*

*The sights*: Downtown Gotebo sits along Commercial Avenue. It is still relatively complete, but its buildings – including a department store – have caved in. The modern school building on 10th Street looks like it could welcome students at any time, until you notice the weeds and locked doors.

*85.Gotebo's department store is now long gone.*

### Cloud Chief (Washita County)

*What's to see*: A school and some cows.

*How to get there*: Drive about 13 miles north of Gotebo on OK 54. Cloud Chief sits just east of the highway along E1216.

*Some history*: Cloud Chief (first named Tacola), was the original county seat of Washita upon its founding during the land run of 1892 on Cheyenne and Arapaho lands. However, voters determined that the nearby town of Cordell was more central, and after a fight with the U.S. Supreme Court, the seat moved there instead.

*The sights*: Cloud Chief was left with a very impressive school building that remained open until 1960, some abandoned infrastructure, and the courthouse's old well.

### Reed (Greer County)

*What's to see*: A large but abandoned church and an old general store.

*How to get there*: Return to Gotebo and follow OK 9 through Hobart. Continue driving west on OK 9 to pass through Lone Wolf (where the railroad tracks approximate the path of the Great Western cattle trail) and Granite. Continue on OK 9 until Reed.

*86.Reed's former general merchandise store.*

*Some history*: Reed is a ranching and farming community that has a cooperative gin, though it never was a big place to begin with. Formerly belonging to Greer County, Texas, Reed opened a post office in the 1890s. Having never attained a right of way for the railroad, the little settlement was unable to maintain its population, which dwindled steadily until the school closed and people began seeking work not in agriculture, but in the cities. Still, Reed can be a happening place, especially during harvesting and planting seasons.

*The sights*: The general store and the large church are very pretty. There's also an abandoned cotton gin that's seen better days.

**By the way: The Greer County War**

The path to Reed is filled with beautiful vistas, courtesy of the Wichita Mountains, original homeland of the Kiowas. Here, the tribe held their Sun Dances, cowboys drove cattle to Dodge City, and outlaws like the Dalton gang hid away from lawmen. It is also the site of the "Greer County War," which pitted Oklahoma against Texas in regards to their respective boundaries. Because the Red River forks into several branches as it reaches into the caprock, its "official" channel, which was supposed to serve as the border between Texas and Indian Territory, was in dispute. Texans believed that the North Fork of the Red River was the actual boundary of the state, and founded Greer County in 1860. At this point, Greer County stretched west from the North Fork of the Red River to the one-hundredth meridian. However, after the Red River wars of 1875, the United States government wanted to resurvey Greer County, which they deemed federal land that could be distributed to railroads and homesteaders. In 1894, the Supreme Court determined that the south branch of the Red River was the intended boundary line as far back as 1819, when the United States negotiated the southern perimeter of the Louisiana Territory with Spain. In one fell swoop, Oklahoma gained over one million acres. Unlike the Kiowas, Comanches, Apaches, and other homesteaders, white ranchers who owned Greer County land when it still belonged to Texas didn't have to endure reserved allotments nor a lottery. Instead, their claims to the land were acknowledged simply for a filing fee.

## Vinson (Harmon County)

*What's to see*: Ruins of an entire town.

*How to get there*: From Reed, simply follow OK 9 west to Vinson.

*Some history*: Vinson was in Greer County, Texas until it wasn't anymore (see Reed for the explanation). Once it became part of Oklahoma, it developed as a town, and seeing that it was pretty much the only sizeable settlement for miles, it became quite large. Founded around 1903, Vinson had with restaurants, cotton gins, stores, gas stations, car dealerships, and a school. It also had party poopers. According to town historians, church ladies and the pastor burned all the pool tables in town to force the men folk to attend church.

*87. Vinson in Harmon County once had a car dealership, a school, a lodge, and even a drive-through to buy beer.*

*The sights*: Commercial buildings, no longer in use, line both sides of OK 9, as does a closed cotton gin. The Masonic Lodge, housed inside a stone structure built by the WPA, seems to be still active. The school consists of a partial foundation, with part of the basement still visible.

This is the end of Oklahoma's Red River Valley Ghost Town Tour!

Determining what is and what isn't a ghost town can be very hard when there aren't any hard and fast rules, especially in a dynamic state like Oklahoma. The history of the former Indian Territory is fraught with land grabs; ethnic enclaves; and legal disputes amid nations, states, and reservations. Coupled with an economy that follows boom and bust cycles, the towns of Oklahoma experienced many ups and downs. For better or for worse, these troubles bring a plethora of exploration options for ghost town hunters.

# Texas Ghost Towns

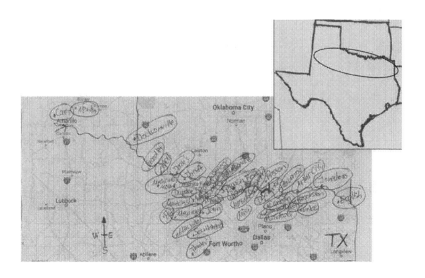

Texas is a big state, so this is a big tour. Since the last tour began from east to west, we'll keep the journey on an east/west trajectory that can be reversed depending on the direction. The tour begins near Texarkana and ends at the birthplace of the Red River, Palo Duro Canyon. The sites include: English, Jonesboro, Arthur City, Brookston, Petty, Enloe, Ravenna, Cannon, Westminster, Valdasta, Dorchester, Preston, Dexter, Marysville, Myra, Bonita, Illinois Bend, Spanish Fort, Belcherville, Ringgold, Stoneburg, Buffalo Springs, Shannon, Antelope, Jean, Southbend, Eliasville, Thurber, Fort Griffin Flat, Megargel, Mankins, Dundee, Thrift, Doan's Crossing, Odell, Thalia, Medicine Mound, Goodlett, Dodson, Carey, and Newlin.

The northern region of Texas reflects a very different history from the rest of the state. The Comancheria (Empire of the Comanches) dominated the western portion of the Red River. Most likely due to the powerful Comanches, the Spanish never colonized their territory. Instead, the majority of European colonizers who settled in North Texas hailed from the western regions of Kentucky, Tennessee, the Carolinas, and Georgia; immigrants from the Arkansas and Missouri territories came to Texas, too. After the Civil War, a large immigrant population arrived from Germany. Interestingly, the majority of north Texas counties did not vote to secede from the Union at the dawn of the Civil War — this may have been because at this point, the economies in North Texas did not rely as much on cotton as counties in East Texas did.

After 1865, the Red River Valley of Texas epitomized the history of the "New South," where cotton shared its industrial might with oil and cattle. The "New South" also reflected North Texas society, as this region was an epicenter for racial violence in the decades after the Civil War. The practice of "spectacle lynching," in which large numbers of whites gathered to watch premeditated, illegal torture executions of African American men, originated in North Texas.

Ultimately, the railroad led North Texas away from its violent roots. In 1872, the Missouri- Kansas- Texas Railroad entered north central Texas, finally connecting the state to northern markets. Considering that steam boat travel on the Red River and other streams in North Texas was hindered by the western drought/flood cycles, man-made transportation avenues rather than natural amenities determined regional growth.

The ghost-town journey through Texas starts at a settlement related to a plantation, then moves towards the west. Notice that the further west one travels, the younger the history gets … and the more remains there are to see. Travelers through Texas will witness verdant prairies, level plains, the Cross Timbers forests, and the famous Texas caprock, a breath-taking landscape that breaks open the prairie into canyons and draws.

### English (Red River County)

*What's to see*: An abandoned store, a pretty church and a restored plantation house.

*How to get there*: From New Boston, go west on US 82 to FM 1699. Follow FM 1699 northwest for about six miles to English. Or, from US 82 just east of Clarksville, take TX 114 northeast for about 14 miles to English.

*Some history*: The eastern portion of Texas' Red River became home to large farming operations that were often considered plantations, even though they did not possess the complete self-sufficiency of traditional plantations. Many grew out of trading posts established in the early 1810s, such as Pecan Point and Wright's Landing (both on private property along the Red River). These trading posts served the men and their families who settled Miller County, Arkansas Territory. In 1824, when Arkansas Territory was divided to form Indian Territory in the west, Miller County was also split and many of the settlers found themselves in Texas. Though many of these settlers swore allegiance to Mexico in order to keep their land, they nonetheless supported the Texas independence movement.

*The sights*: English began its life as the plantation of Oliver English, who came to Texas in 1840. His estate grew cotton, which he shipped to Jefferson, Texas via the Red River. The little hamlet that grew around his operation is notable because his house has been restored, and a small store, now abandoned, still remains. The 1865 church and cemetery are worth a visit.

### By the way: Old Boston, Boston, and New Boston

For a brief stint, Dekalb served as the first county seat when Bowie County was founded in 1840. Soon, the seat shifted to Boston, a town settled in the late 1820s which was more centrally located. When the Texas and Pacific Railway announced plans to bring its track through the county in the

*89.Boston's former jail, between Old Boston and New Boston in Bowie County.*

mid-1880s, the proposed right of way was a few miles north of Boston. To not lose its status as the county seat, several of the town's citizens and businesses moved to meet the route. Boston became Old Boston, and the new location, approved in 1891, co-opted the name Boston, where a large courthouse and jail anchored the new downtown. When the tracks were actually laid, they missed downtown by a mile to the north. Businesses moved away from downtown towards the railroad, and the new downtown commercial district that centered on the depot became known as New Boston. A fire destroyed the courthouse in the 1980s, and instead of rebuilding in the Boston section, the new courthouse was built along Interstate 30 in the New Boston section. Now, the county seat of Bowie County has two ghost towns in its midst – Old Boston, of which nothing is left, and Boston, which still displays the imposing remains of its two story, sturdy jail. The old jail sits at the corner of Walters and Merrill streets.

### Jonesboro (Red River County)

*What's to see*: A roadside memorial that includes an old gravestone and a Texas historical marker.

*How to get there*: From Clarksville, go north on TX SH 37 to Albion, an old ferry crossing at the Red River. At Albion, turn west onto FM 195 and follow for about five miles to FM 410 at Woodland. Go northeast on FM 410 for several miles until you see the site on the northwestern side of the road, near the Red River.

*Some history*: Jonesboro was once quite a large settlement that served as a ferry crossing and port on the Red River. Founded circa 1815 by its namesake, Henry Jones, the town was a regional hub and even served, albeit briefly, as the

Miller County (Arkansas) seat. In 1843, a huge flood destroyed most of the town's docks and buildings. The Red River shifted as well, and without access to the stream, the town did not rebuild.

*The sights*: Today, all that remains is a lone grave marker that was found by a farmer plowing his field, which is displayed at the roadside memorial. Unfortunately, the scant remains of Jonesboro are now on private land and are inaccessible to the ghost town hunter.

### Arthur City (Lamar County)

*What's to see*: Not much, but it's one of the few towns in Texas located directly on the shores of the Red River.

*How to get there*: From Jonesboro, go west/south on FM 410 back to FM 195. Go west on FM 195 to Novice. In Novice, take FM 2648 west until it ends at US 271. Turn north on US 271 and follow it six miles to Arthur City, which sits just south of the Red River bridge on the west side of the road.

*Some history*: Though Arthur City was platted in 1886 for the St. Louis and San Francisco Railway, the location along the river saw earlier history. Caddo villages lined the shores before Europeans arrived. In the 1830s, Samuel Fulton, who also founded Fulton, Arkansas along the Red River (see page 95), set up a steamboat operation close by. Cargo shipping favored the efficiency of railroads over steamboats, and Arthur City became the site for tourist excursion trips before river travel ultimately halted. At one point, Arthur City had a school, a few cotton gins, a telegraph office, a hotel, several stores, and a saw mill. Today, the several businesses and churches still call Arthur City home, but it's no longer a busy little town along the river by the tracks. The railroad has become a tourist relic as well. Whenever funds are available, an excursion train runs between Paris, Texas and Hugo, Oklahoma.

*90.A creative use of an old SUV to use as a storm shelter peeks out from the brush in Arthur City.*

*The sights*: Some non-descript businesses line the town's main street, which parallels the railroad tracks. Behind the tracks are weed strewn roads and a few houses. The first street in Arthur City past the railroad tracks ends at the Red River, with a good vantage point of the Frisco Railway's iron truss bridge.

### Brookston (Lamar County)
*What's to see*: Not much.
*How to get there*: Go west of Paris on US 82, then turn south onto FM 38. Follow the road into Brookston.
*Some history*: Established in 1870 as a temporary terminus for the Texas and Pacific Railway, Brookston once had the

distinction of being the largest exporter of hay to feed horses during the Great War (1914-1919). Brookston was a fairly active community, even with a saloon, but the loss of train traffic, the Great Depression, and the re-routing of US 82 a mile north of town, put a stop to all of that.

*The sights*: Several homes surrounding the post office used to be gas stations and stores. Ruins lie in the woods south of the tracks.

## Petty (Lamar County)

*91.The floor and the vault from a bank are all that's left of downtown Petty.*

*What's to see*: Remains of a bank.

*How to get there*: Follow FM 38, which parallels the old right-of-way of the Texas and Pacific Railway in Brookston. This road turns into FM 1508, which takes you to Petty. This road is also the old alignment of US 82. Make sure to slow down to appreciate the stone culverts at the railroad trestles along the road.

*Some history*: Petty's location on a small rise made it a very early and popular spot for pre-Civil War farmers and the post-Civil War Texas and Pacific Railway. The town steadily grew in both population and businesses, with a cotton gin, a grist mill, and a furniture maker. Like Brookston, the Great Depression took its toll and Petty lost its businesses. Its stark white, homey churches attest to the town's former prominence.

*What's to see*: At the intersection of the railroad track and FM 137 on the west side of town sits the remains of a once grand bank. Its bricked vault still stands.

### By the way: US 82

US 82 travels from Georgia to New Mexico and, in the Red River Valley, parallels Spanish trading paths that connected New Spain provinces to El Paso and Santa Fe. During the Republic of Texas (1836-1845), a trading expedition led by Mexican and American merchants used the paths and marketed the route as the Chihuahua Trail to connect their trade. When highways were named rather than numbered, the road was known as, rather uninspired, as the North Texas Road.

### Enloe (Delta County)

*What's to see*: An entire downtown.

*How to get there*: Drive south on TX 24 from Paris to Cooper, the Delta County seat. From Cooper, take TX SH 24 northeast to FM 2949. Turn north onto FM 2949 and follow it into Enloe.

*Some history*: Enloe, originally settled in the 1880s, was never a big town, but it did gain some prominence in the surrounding area when the Texas and Midland Railroad passed through in 1897. Within a few decades, the town had a sizeable population, schools, banks, general stores, a cotton gin, and a lumber company. But people are fickle. After trains stopped coming through and work opportunities enticed residents to move, the town diminished, and eventually lost its school.

*The sights*: Although a few hundred residents remain, the entire downtown is now abandoned save for a little museum and a bee keeper who sells bottles of honey inside a store front.

### Ravenna (Fannin County)

*What's to see*: Abandoned buildings and a missing church (well, it used to be there, and I miss it).

*How to get there*: From Bonham (Fannin County seat), take US 82 west to FM 898. Turn north on FM 898. The road will bend towards the east. Next, turn north onto FM 274 and follow it for about ten miles to Ravenna.

*Some history*: Known as Willow Point before the Civil War, town founders applied for a post office in the 1880s and named the town Ravenna. By then, the town had several businesses, including mills, and was able to entice the Denison, Bonham and New Orleans Railroad to lay tracks (this line would later become the Missouri- Kansas- Texas Railroad). However, rail service ceased by 1929. Businesses closed, and within twenty years, Ravenna's schools were shut down. In 1965, a fire destroyed much of downtown.

Although Ravenna still has a post office and a city hall, it is less than half the town it used to be.

*The sights*: An old gas station, a brick building from the turn of the century, and a few sturdy houses hint at Ravenna's past. Even the right-of-way for the railroad is no longer discernable. The wooden Christian Church from the 1870s, once the pride of Ravenna, has been either demolished or moved.

### Cannon (Grayson County)

*What's to see*: An old church and a very interesting cemetery.

*How to get there*: From Sherman (Grayson County seat), travel TX SH 11 southeast for about 15 miles to Tom Bean. Once in Tom Bean, turn south on Britton Street, west on King Street, and south onto FM 2729 towards Van Alstyne. Follow FM 2729 to its end in Cannon.

*Some history*: Established in the 1850s, Cannon was named after planter and slaver Elijah Cannon, who came from South Carolina and established the town surrounding his farm. Cannon was a stop on a stage coach line that linked Sherman to McKinney and thus grew into a sizeable community, but all was lost when the Houston and Texas Central Railway decided to place its route west and founded Van Alstyne. Cannon quickly fell by the wayside.

*The sights*: Fragments of the community remain, including a wooden Methodist church built in 1896, some older structures that may have had commercial uses, and the cemetery. This cemetery is segregated, with the races separated by a small lane. The white section, founded before the Civil War, features the impressive graves of the Cannon family, plus a few wooden tombstones next to the Cannon plot that most likely denote burials of enslaved people. The black section, which was inaugurated after freedom, also include wooden tombstones. These belong to the Billy and Glory Boyd, an emancipated couple who were the first burials in the black section in 1880.

### Westminster (Collin County)

*What's to see*: Abandoned buildings but a fairly active downtown.

*How to get there*: From Cannon, go west on FM 121 into Van Alstyne. Once there, turn south onto Waco Street/ TX SH 5 and follow this road all the way to TX SH 121. Turn northeast on TX SH 121 to FM 2862. Turn north on FM 2862 and follow it into Westminster. Coming from McKinney (Collin County seat), drive north on US 75/69, then take TX SH 121 northeast past Melissa. Turn north on FM 2862 and follow it into town.

*Some history*: Westminster is one of two "newest" ghost towns on the Texas list. In 1988, its school district disbanded, and in 2005, citizens voted to dis-incorporate it to forgive state tax burdens. To top it off, in 2006 a tornado, which registered as a very destructive F3, left three people dead, adding additional pain to the hurt. Originally named Seven

Points, its growth began when Westminster College was established in 1895. Gradually, the little town attracted more people, including many farmers. An interurban train came through town to link Westminster to neighboring communities like Whitewright and Greenville. However, the big railroads bypassed the town. The population dwindled over the years. Proximity to burgeoning southern Collin County and Dallas County kept Westminster from completely disappearing, and today, it's still well-populated. Westminster continually risks being annexed by Melissa or Anna, two nearby settlements whose growths have skyrocketed with the influx of people moving to the Dallas-Fort Worth Metroplex. Although it still exists on maps and road signs, legally Westminster is a non-entity.

*The sights*: Westminster's downtown has a number of abandoned commercial buildings but still has two open businesses: one is a motorcycle hang-out. Over the past few years, the little town has attracted bikers from all around who like the area's scenic, winding roads.

### Valdasta (Collin County)

*What's to see*: An elementary school.

*How to get there*: From Westminster, go south on FM 2862 until it ends at FM 545. Turn west onto FM 545, then turn south onto Old Valdasta Road.

*Some history*: Valdasta, which sits prominently on a scenic hillside, has been a small farming community since its founding in 1886. Until the mid- twentieth century, it remained fairly busy, with several stores, three churches, and a sturdy, brick school. As population shifted away to nearby urban centers, the school and eventually, the stores closed.

*The sights*: The former Valdasta school still stands, but is now home to a small but nosey cattle herd. The cozy wooden chapel for the Baptist Church sits next to the old school and still greets visitors on Sundays.

94.*Former school of Valdasta, which was the pride of the community when it was built. A 1920's newspaper article touted its strong storm shelter.*

### Dorchester (Grayson County)

*What's to see*: Disused commercial buildings.

*How to get there*: From Valdasta, go west on FM 545 to TX 121. Turn west/south on TX 121, then proceed to travel north on TX 5. TX 5 traverses the tidy railroad communities of Melissa, Anna, Van Alstyne, and Howe. Just north of Howe, turn west onto FM 902 and follow it to Dorchester.

*Some history*: Established along the St. Louis, San Francisco and Texas Railway route in the late nineteenth century, Dorchester remained a small town until it got even smaller with its population losses due to nearby bigger cities, though it still has an active city hall. Prior to the town's founding, the main north/south road through Dorchester was an emigrant road and the famed Shawnee Cattle Trail.

*The sights*: A strip of commercial buildings, long abandoned, remain in the town's center. Trains still go through Dorchester, and still stop at the grain silos.

### By the way: The Shawnee Trail

Prior to the Civil War, Texas ranchers drove their cattle east to New Orleans, where steamboats took the herds to slaughterhouses up the Mississippi River. When the railroads reached as far west as Sedalia, Missouri in the late 1850s, the Texas cattlemen trailed their herds to the northern railheads instead. The drover's route became known as the Shawnee Trail, as it crossed Shawneetown along the Red River in Grayson County. The trail parallels today's TX 289, an old Indian trading path that was known in the nineteenth century as the Texas Emigrant Trail, the Texas Cattle Road, or Preston Road.

### Preston (Grayson County)

*What's to see*: Just a cemetery, but there's a lot of history buried in this cemetery.

*How to get there*: From Dorchester, travel west on FM 902 to TX 289/ Preston Road. Travel north on TX 289 for about 20 miles until it dead ends at a cemetery on the shores of Lake Texoma.

*Some history*: The town of Preston was built around Holland Coffee's trading post, which he established in the 1840s after abandoning the Petersburg trading post further west. Coffee traded with Choctaws and Chickasaws across the river in Indian Territory as well as ransomed kidnapped people from the Comanches to sell back to their families or owners for a profit. The Texas legislature investigated him for this practice, but his friendship with Sam Houston gave him much leeway. He was ultimately appointed an Indian Agent and served in the Texas legislature.

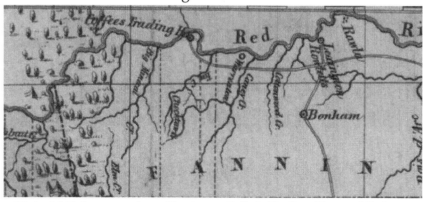

96.An 1840s' era map shows Preston as Coffee's Trading House while it was still in Fannin, not Grayson, County. The map also shows a few towns that no longer exist, such as Lexington and Warrenton (aka Warren) (LOC).

Holland Coffee had a very unique name with an identity that epitomized many of the frontier-people who settled early Texas — a contrarian nature. Coffee, for example, may have had a hand in the killing of John Hart, a Fannin County sheriff, over a land dispute.

Holland Coffee himself met a violent end. He married Sophia Auginbaugh (nee Suttenfield) for whom he and his enslaved people built a plantation named Glen Eden. Sophia was also one of these Texan characters whose past was a little suspect — she may have been a "camp follower" during the Texas revolution. When a trader at Preston made a disparaging remark to that effect, Holland Coffee defended her honor but lost his life. Sophia would go on to marry George Butts and then James Porter, all the while residing at Glen Eden.

97.*Preston doesn't exist anymore save for this 1936 stone marker, its cemetery... and a Pet Cemetery (key the Ramones here).*

*The sights*: Holland, Sophia, and her last husband, James, are buried in the Preston cemetery. The cemetery is not in its original location, however. Workers for the Works Progress Administration workers moved the bodies and markers in the late 1930s in preparation for the construction of the Denison dam at the confluence of the Red and Washita rivers. The building of the dam meant that Preston would be drowned to make way for Lake Texoma. To save the history of the settlement, Grayson County citizens disassembled several Preston buildings, including Glen Eden, in the hopes of reconstructing them at a city park. Unfortunately, Glen Eden's remains burned before they could be resurrected, but many of Preston's former buildings have been reconstructed and can be visited in Frontier Village at Loy Lake Park on US 75 just north of Sherman.

### Dexter (Cooke County)

*What's to see*: A few abandoned buildings in the brush.

*How to get there*: Return to US 82/ TX 56 from Preston, then head west. Turn north onto FM 678 towards Callisburg. Continue on FM 678 past Callisburg until the road ends at Dexter.

*Some history*: Dexter began life after the Civil War near a fresh water spring. Its location was also straight west, as the crow flew, from the newly established town of Denison. The founding of Denison by the Missouri- Kansas- Texas Railroad ushered in a railroad boom, and citizens were hopeful that the same railroad, when building west, would make a beeline towards their town. To that end, several hotels, businesses, mills, banks, and lodges appeared, and it seemed as if Dexter would surpass Gainesville as Cooke County's biggest town. Alas, Dexter's plans did not come to fruition. The Missouri- Kansas- Texas Railroad built instead towards the southwest to link with Whitesboro, and it eventually reached into Gainesville and beyond. And just as quickly as it emerged, Dexter faded away.

*98.Dexter's former bank vault.*

*The sights*: Today, not much remains of Dexter save for a little church, two graveyards, a few chimneys, and the hulks of formerly solid buildings that have become overgrown with oak trees. Crashing through the brush reveals a brick vault, once part of the bank, hidden behind trees between the church and the burned building hulk.

### Marysville (Cooke County)

*What's to see*: A school, an old store, and a cemetery.

*How to get there*: From Dexter, return to US 82/ TX 56 and head west through Gainesville and Lindsay. Turn north onto FM 2739 and follow it until it ends. At the "T" in the road, turn to the east onto FM 421, then turn north onto FM 417. Follow this road all the way to the Marysville Baptist Church. The school is east of the church on FM 462. Please note that many of these roads are unpaved and may be tricky in wet weather.

*Some history*: This little farming community may not seem

 like much today, and even when it was alive and kicking, it was never really a happening place. However, the school building is a very real, historical testament to how communities in the Red River Valley began. Building public schools was not easy when funds were not available — and for most people in the Southwest, access to cash was always very limited. To address these needs, local Freemasons built lodges for their communities to act as school houses during the week, a place to get away from their wives on Saturdays, and as churches on Sundays.

*The sights*: These small but sturdy testaments to literacy and civic-mindedness can be seen all over Cooke and Montague Counties – we'll be visiting another one in Illinois Bend.

### Myra (Cooke County)

*What's to see*: Some downtown buildings and the old right-of-way for the Missouri- Kansas- Texas Railroad.

*How to get there*: From Marysville, return to US 82. Just west of Lindsay on US 82 is FM 1198. Follow this road south for about a mile to Myra.

*Some history*: Myra is a railroad town. It was founded in the late 1880s along the Gainesville, Henrietta and Western Railway line, which would later become the Missouri-

Kansas- Texas Railroad. In the ensuing years, Myra grew into a sizeable settlement, especially when oil was discovered nearby. Myra could boast a telephone company, electric company, a hospital, several businesses, its own school district, and more. Interestingly, it was not the railroad that killed Myra, but the highway. When US 82 was straightened in the 1930s, the new road bed bypassed the town, and within thirty years, Myra lost its railroad, school, and hospital.

*100.Myra's ice house may have been a bank vault in its previous life.*

*The sights*: Today, a playground has replaced most of Myra's downtown, though the old drug store is still standing. An ice house — possibly used as a jail as well — stands on the eastern side of the main road. If you follow the original alignment of US 82 (west on Bradford Street, then north on Bergman Street, which then bends to towards the west again), you'll parallel the old railroad line for a bit. Although the tracks are gone, their right-of-way provides a good visualization of the effect the railroads had for communities like Myra.

## Bonita (Montague County)

*What's to see*: Lots of destruction next to the Baptist Church, and several foundations.

*How to get there*: From Myra, drive west on US 82 past Muenster and St. Jo. Turn north on FM 1815. Bonita is less than a mile on this road.

*Some history*: Bonita was a stop on the Gainesville, Henrietta and Western Railway line (it would later become the Missouri- Kansas- Texas Railroad.) Like Myra, US 82 bypassed the little town during the renewal project, and Bonita gradually lost its population.

*The sights*: All that's left of old Bonita are some nifty ruins inside a destroyed building, foundations with stairs to nowhere, and a few farms.

## Illinois Bend (Montague County)

*What's to see*: A stone church, a nicely restored school, and some outhouses.

*How to get there*: From Bonita, you can drive north on FM 1815 until it ends at FM 1956. Turn east on FM 1956 to Capps Corner. At Capps Corner, turn north onto FM 677. This will take you to Illinois Bend. Or you can follow FM 373 north from Muenster (Cooke County) to FM 677.

*Some history*: This small town was founded before the Civil War as Wardville, but began to grow afterwards, once it received permission to open a post office. Like in Marysville, the Freemasons built the lodge that would also function as a school; other buildings followed.

*The sights*: The school, now restored, still stands behind the 1939 Nazarene church. While the town never became anything more than a simple farming community, Illinois

Bend's location is absolutely idyllic and serene. While you're there, enjoy finding the few outhouses scattered around the remains of the community.

*101.Lovely little school at Illinois Bend.*

### Spanish Fort (Montague County)

*What's to see*: Abandoned high school, interesting cemetery, old buildings, and lots of discarded things.

*How to get there*: From Illinois Bend, drive west on FM 677 until it turns north. Instead of following FM 677, continue west on FM 2953. At the "T," turn north onto FM 103 to drive to Spanish Fort. Or, you can go north, then west on FM 103 to Spanish Fort from Nocona (Montague County, on US 82).

*Some history*: Spanish Fort is one of the best-known ghost towns in Texas, and with good reason. Its existence began very early. In the mid-eighteenth century, the town was the site of a massive fortified village, spanning the Red River on both sides. The Taovayans, relatives to the Wichitas, lived here, and Comanche, Kiowa, French, Comanchero, and American, and Spanish traders visited frequently. The

Spanish called the fort on the north side of the river San Bernardo, and San Teodoro on the southern side.

*102.One of the last remaining downtown buildings at Spanish Fort.*

In 1758, Comanche and Taovayan warriors led a raid on the Santa Cruz de San Saba Mission near today's Menard in central Texas, in which seventeen friars were killed. The Comanches and Taovayans were exacting revenge on the Spanish, who had become friendly with the Apaches. The Apaches actually urged the friars to build the mission, knowing full well that this would draw the Comanche ire. Apparently, the Apaches hoped that the Spanish and Comanches would kill each other, thus leaving the Apaches the ultimate victors.

Under Diego Ortiz Parilla, over one hundred men marched to the forts to confront the Comanches and Taovayans, but they quickly found themselves outnumbered and retreated. Soon, however, the trade at the fort diminished due to disease and warfare. In the 1830s, Holland Coffee erected a new trading post on the site of San

Bernardo, but he was stopped by the federal government because he did not have permission to set up trade in Indian Territory. He left to start a trading post further east in today's Grayson County, which he named Preston (see page 185).

103.An 1824 *map of Mexican Texas points to the Pawnee village that would later become Spanish Fort (David Rumsey).*

When Americans came to the old fort in the 1870s, they first named their new town site Burlington. However, settlers began to find trade goods and earthen dams from the old trading post, and mistook them for debris from a "Spanish fort." They changed the name of their settlement to reflect their theory.

Just like its predecessor, the town of Spanish Fort became a trading center, especially for cowboys driving cattle across the river into Indian Territory up the famous Chisholm Trail. Though they crossed at Red River Station west of Spanish Fort – an official crossing manned by livestock agents who checked the cattle for ticks that transmitted Texas fever – cowboys came into Spanish Fort to gamble, visit, buy provisions, and relax before going up the trail. Hotels and saloons welcomed the men, as did

 prostitutes and card sharps. The lawlessness of Indian Territory spilled over frequently into Spanish Fort. Though violence was not uncommon, Spanish Fort could be respectable, too. Two newspapers were published in the town, and H. J. Justin, a boot maker from Indiana, opened a shop in Spanish Fort to supply cowboys with custom-made boots.

Like with most towns along the Red River, the boom-days did not last long. The railroad bypassed Spanish Fort, and cattle trails opened further west. By the early twentieth century, Spanish Fort was on its way to doom. It rebounded briefly when wildcatters discovered oil in the region. A large brick school was erected in 1924 to accommodate the influx of new families; however, the oil boom quickly diminished, and finally, Spanish Fort became a ghost town once again. *The sights*: The school and cemetery, many with hand-carved tomb stones, sit on FM 103 west of Spanish Fort. A lone, brick store stands along the main thoroughfare, across from a Texas historical marker that commemorates Spanish Fort's history. Many abandoned buildings dot the town, though it still has some residents.

*105.Spanish Fort's former high school reflects the town's oil wealth in the first part of the 20ᵗʰ century.*

## Belcherville (Montague County)

*What's to see*: A few abandoned buildings, scattered around a few streets.

*How to get there*: From Spanish Fort, go west, then south, on FM 103 to Nocona. In Nocona, turn west onto US 82 and follow it to FM 1816. Follow FM 1816 briefly to Belcherville.

*Some history*: Before 1860, the site that would become the town of Belcherville was simply a ranch headquarters for the Belcher family. But when the Gainesville, Henrietta, and Western Railway (soon to be bought out by the Missouri-Kansas- Texas Railroad) laid tracks through the ranch, the Belchers plotted a small town and in 1893, Belcherville was incorporated. Lots of cattle business came through, and for about twenty years Belcherville did well, even boasting two schools. But two fires destroyed much of the town, and as the cattle drives subsided, so did the town. Rail service ended by 1969, and now Belcherville is almost devoid of people.

*The sights*: Very little remains of the town save for a few scattered ruins and a non-descript, unused service station.

### By the way: The Tales N Trails Museum

Along US 82 on the east side of the town of Nocona sit two important Texas historical sites: the former Nocona Boot Company building, rendered in beautiful art deco architecture from what was once a Sears store, and the very informative Tales N Trails Museum. When the railroad bypassed the town of Spanish Fort, H.J. Justin relocated his boot making facility to Nocona. After taking over the business, Justin's son moved the factory towards Fort Worth. Justin's daughter Enid, however, herself a renowned boot maker, remained in Nocona, and the Nocona Boot Company was born. It became the town's largest employer and benefactor, as did the ranchers in the area. One of these ranchers, Joe Benton, amassed a large collection of Native American artifacts that became the seed for the *Tales N Trails Museum*, which his daughter, Clarice, helped to found. The museum holds a fantastic collection of aboriginal artifacts and leather works.

### Ringgold (Montague County)

*What's to see*: An abandoned downtown.

*How to get there*: From Belcherville, continue west on US 82. Ringold is in the northwest corner where US 82 intersects with US 81. To get to Ringold's downtown, turn north on Loop 19 and follow it into town.

*Some history*: Normally, towns that still have active schools cannot be considered ghost towns... unless they are. Ringold is a good example of this because it used to be much bigger and much more important. Two railroads and two national roads bisected in this hamlet, which should have ensured Ringold's survival. But wild fires and tornados put a real hurt on the town. Its elementary school is still there, sharing students with nearby Stoneburg, where the high school is located.

*106.A downtown remain in Ringgold.*

The town began when the Missouri- Kansas- Texas Railroad (MKT) bisected the Chicago, Rock Island and Pacific Railroad (CRIP) in the early 1890s. Joe Harris, a prominent cattle rancher, bought up the land surrounding the intersection to sell as town sites, and Ringgold — originally called Harrisonia — quickly became a major market town. Several smaller villages in the area abandoned their sites to move to the soon-to-be city. All was going well until the MKT ceased operations in the early 1970s. Although the CRIP still came through, it no longer stopped. People began moving away to find work and opportunity elsewhere. The death knell to Ringgold's sad fate was sealed by a horrific outbreak of wildfires in 2006. The fire was so intense that it consumed most of the town within fifteen minutes, creating "fire tornados," The destruction could be seen from NASA's satellite. Ringgold's neighbor, Stoneburg, suffered a similar fate in 2009.

*The sights*: The Gold-Burg elementary school is still active, and several residents rebuilt after the wild fire. However, the core of the town is deserted. A calaboose sits behind the row of still-standing buildings along the town's main street. The impressive but sad remains of a large wooden Methodist church sit on 3rd street across from the school.

### Stoneburg (Montague County)

107.A *beautiful former gas station made of petrified wood and molten glass in Stoneburg.*

*What's to see*: A hollowed-out gas station faced with petrified wood.

*How to get there*: From Ringgold, go south on US 81 to Stoneburg.

*Some history*: Like Ringgold, Stoneburg suffered a major fire that gutted its downtown. Due to the 2009 inferno, all of the buildings from Stoneburg's downtown core have been destroyed. Now, even though this little hamlet is home to the impressive high school campus of the Gold-Burg ISD, its loss of commercial activity places it squarely in the ghost town category.

Stoneburg was established when the Chicago, Rock Island and Pacific Railroad built their tracks alongside an emigrant and cattle trail in the 1890s. In the early twentieth century, the road became part of a national highway system, designated as Highway #2 or the Meridian Highway (see page 148).

*The sights*: Proximity to this major road allowed entrepreneurs in Stoneburg to build several gas stations, one of which survives, in ghost town form, on the east side of the highway south of the high school. Faced with petrified wood and chunks of glass from a glass manufacturing facility, the two-story gas station is now just a shell, but a very pretty one.

### Buffalo Springs (Clay County)

*What's to see*: Homesteader cabins, some stone buildings, and a gym.

*How to get there*: From Stoneburg, return to Bowie on US 81. As US 81 jogs south on the north side of town, turn onto

West Wise Street/ FM 174. Continue west on this road to Buffalo Springs.

*Some history*: Named after a bison wallow, Buffalo Springs began as an attempt to organize a farming community during the Civil War. Raids by Comanches forced the site to be abandoned. The wooden stockade built by the early settlers almost convinced the U.S. government to build a military fort here, but Jacksboro (further south) got the nod

*108.Picturesque pioneer abode in Buffalo Springs.*

instead. By 1878, another civilian attempt at settlement was more successful. The town grew relatively rapidly, but lack of continuous good water and distance to the railroads did not allow the settlement to grow into anything substantial. *The sights*: The aridness of the area has allowed many of the early, wooden homesteads to remain erect, leading to delightful vistas in the spring time. The town's school and gym were built with WPA labor during the Great Depression. Only the gym, now fenced off and overgrown, remains.

### Shannon (Clay County)

*What's to see*: A sturdy vault.

*How to get there*: From Buffalo Springs, go west on FM 174 to TX 148. Turn south onto TX 148 for about five miles. Then, head west on FM 175 to a little bitty place called Shannon.

*Some history*: A contemporary of Buffalo Springs, the now non-existent town of Shannon originally was called, quite poetically, Stampede Springs. It was apparently renamed in honor of an Irish pioneer family. Once again, the lack of the railroad led to the town's demise.

*The sights*: Along what was once the center of town on FM 175 sits a bank vault, surrounded by remains of the foundation.

### Antelope (Jack County)

*What's to see*: A cute, former downtown and a school.

*How to get there*: Continue west on FM 175 to the intersection with TX/Spur 187. Turn south on Spur 187. Antelope sits on this small spur, which was once the original US Highway 281 until new highway construction bypassed the town.

*Some history*: Established in 1858, the town centered on ranching. It continued to do so after the Civil War – Antelope's general stores supplied cattle drives, served as a daily stage coach stop, built a cotton gin, and remained a hub for area farmers and ranchers. Once again, the lack of a railroad hindered the town's growth. By the mid- twentieth century, the school had closed, and very few businesses remained opened.

*What's to see*: A beautiful stone building, erected in the 1880s, was once a general store. Along the side of the store is School House Road. Follow this road to see the old school, which is now the town's community center. The WPA built the gym.

### Jean (Young County)

*What's to see*: Abandoned downtown.

*How to get there*: From Antelope, go south on US 281 to FM 1191. Turn south-west onto FM 1191 and follow it to TX 114. Head west on TX 114 to arrive at Jean.

*Some history*: Jean was a small ranching center that grew into a larger settlement when the Gulf, Texas and Western Railroad came through. Named after the first postmaster's sweetheart, Jean's growth was managed by the Trinity Townsite Company, a consortium that invested in buying, then platting and selling, town lots along railroad lines. As usual, Jean's importance diminished once train traffic stopped.

*The sights*: In downtown Jean, you'll find remains of its bank, several store fronts, and a wooden store. The old school on

Buchanan Street (a few blocks northwest of Jean's Main Street) is now a community center.

*110.Pretty Jean.*

## By the way: Fort Richardson

Further south of Antelope on US 281 sits Jacksboro, home to Fort Richardson State Park. Fort Richardson is an Indian-Wars era fortification with lots of history along Lost Creek. To secure the Great Plains to new development, the U.S. government had allotted reservations in Indian Territory for the southern Plains tribes through the Medicine Lodge Creek Treaties of 1867. However, not all of the Kiowas and Comanches agreed to abide by the treaties, and they continued to stage raids on settlers and drovers. Fort Richardson was built in 1868 in response to these conflicts. After a horrific attack on teamsters along Salt Creek in 1871, which General William Tecumseh Sherman had narrowly avoided, Fort Richardson became the stage area to finalize defeat of the Comancheria. First, Kiowa leaders were put on trial at Jacksboro for their roles in the murders of the teamsters. Then, Major Ranald S. McKenzie waged war against famed Indian chiefs Quanah Parker of the Comanches and Geronimo of the Lipan Apaches. Defeat came at Palo Duro Canyon in 1874, after McKenzie slaughtered over a thousand Indian horses. The Southern Plains Indians were forced into the white man's world.

### By the way: The Goodnight-Loving Trail

In Young County, TX SH 114 parallels the Goodnight-Loving Trail, which was blazed in the late 1860s by Oliver Loving and Charles Goodnight to bring cattle to ranches in New Mexico and Colorado.

### Fort Belknap (Young County)

*What's to see*: A pre-Civil War fort with lots of history and intact buildings. Also, an interesting cemetery.

*How to get there*: From Jean, travel south on FM 1769 to US 380. Turn west on US 380 to get to Newcastle. Follow US 380 to FM 61, which will take you right to Fort Belknap.

*Some history*: Established in 1851, Texas' northern-most outpost, situated near the Brazos River, served to protect Americans from Comanche raids. It quickly became a center of commerce and protection, with many smaller tribes seeking refuge from both the Comanches and the American settlers, and stage coaches and emigrant trails leading to the post.

Fort Belknap was also the head station for the short-lived Brazos Indian Reservation. In the 1850s, the United States established a reservation in Young County to house displaced Texan tribes like the Caddos, Wichitas,

Tawakonis, Tayovayans, and Cherokees (who came to Texas with Sam Houston). The peaceful Penateka Comanches also received a reserve in nearby Throckmorton County. In actuality, the reservation served as a "buffer" between the Comancheria and American settlers, and it was the reservation Indians who suffered the brunt of attacks by hostile Comanches as well as hostile Texans. However, Texans accused the reservation Indians of collaborating with Comanches and Mexicans to ferment troubles. John Baylor, former Indian Agent at the Comanche Reservation and editor of the anti-Indian newspaper, *The White Man*, gathered a militia to fight the Indians, killing two people who were plowing their fields. After this altercation, Robert Neighbors, the U.S. Indian Agent ultimately in charge of the reservations, ordered the tribes to be removed to Indian Territory. Neighbors openly accused American Texans of fabricating conspiracies and blowing incidents of depredations out of proportion. He was shot dead at Fort Belknap in 1859 by Edward Cornett and was buried in the civilian cemetery at the fort.

The United States surrendered the fort to Texas during the Civil War. It then served as a gathering point for Texas Rangers who were charged with protecting the frontier against Indian raids. After the Red River Wars against the southern Plains Indians in 1875, the fort was no longer needed and fell into disuse. It was repaired in many citizen-led programs from the 1930s until the 1980s and is now a museum and park.

*The sights*: Much of the original compound has been restored and is available for daily viewing. The fort's very interesting museum displays a plethora of artifacts. A fantastic picnic area can be found underneath a huge arbor covered in grapevines. The cemetery is worth a visit for its interesting array of tombstones, including that of Robert Neighbors.

### Southbend (Young County)

*What's to see*: Remains of town and an abandoned hotel. Also, a bridge to nowhere.

*How to get there*: From Fort Belknap, continue driving south on FM 61 to Graham (Young County seat). Next, go south on TX 67 to South Bend, which sits just to the west of the road on the Brazos River on FM 701.

*Some history*: Southbend began in the late nineteenth century as a farm and ranch center and boomed briefly in the 1920s due to oil. However, oil discoveries were few and far, and instead, the hot mineral waters coming from the oil drilling sites led the town to advertise itself as a resort. The Chicago, Rock Island and Gulf Railway built a line through Southbend to take advantage of the tourist traffic, which ebbed to a mere trickle by the 1950s. Now, Southbend is just another ghost town, but with plenty of remains.

*The sights*: The shells of cabins belonging to a roadside motor court can be viewed along FM 701. On South Main Street are some derelict commercial buildings. The abutments of the bridge on the Chicago, Rock Island and Pacific Railway grace North Main Street.

### Eliasville (Young County)

*What's to see*: An entire town and an abandoned mill.

*How to get there*: From Southbend, follow FM 701 southwest to Eliasville. Elm Creek, a tributary of the Brazos River, crosses the path twice — at the second crossing stand the remains of a truss bridge beside the newer, concrete structure.

*111.One of the only extant historic mills in North Texas is in Eliasville.*

*Some history*: Like Southbend, Eliasville, nestled in gentle hills at the extreme southern end of Young County, discovered that the hot mineral waters, coupled with scenic vistas, are a great way to encourage tourist traffic. The Chicago, Rock Island and Gulf Railway thought so, too, and built a line to Eliasville's resorts in the early twentieth century. But Eliasville developed much earlier. Already in the 1870s, it boasted a major flour mill, a school, and several businesses, and continued to grow well into the 1950s. Several bridges crossed Gage Creek, and at least two churches overlooked their flocks on College Heights. Today, however, Eliasville is a shadow of what it once was. Tourists are notoriously fickle, and nearby Mineral Wells (Palo Pinto County) siphoned many because of its grand Baker Hotel.

*The sights*: As you come into town, notice the old school building on the south side of the road, which was turned into a private residence. Several churches, some still in use, line College Heights Street. As FM 701 winds down a hill, you'll enter what is left of downtown Eliasville. Several abandoned buildings occupy both sides of the road. The bridge across Gage Creek offers a beautiful view of the old Donnell Mill, which was rebuilt in the late 1920s after a fire destroyed most of it. A few abutments from former bridges can be discerned on the northern side of the creek.

### Thurber (Erath County)

*What's to see*: A huge chimney, ice house, abandoned tracks, and other ruins of this once-thriving town. The cemetery and museum are worth an extensive visit.

*How to get there*: From Eliasville in Young County, go south on FM 701 to TX 67. Turn south on TX 67, then turn east on US 180 (this is the old Bankhead Highway). You will drive past Caddo and Brad and several pretty mountains. Then, you'll turn south on TX 16 to Strawn. In Strawn, turn east on FM 108, past Mingus, to Thurber. If you are coming from Fort Worth, simply take I-20 west to Thurber. Or, if you have the time — and the advice is to: go ahead and take the time — travel I-20 west to Weatherford. In Weatherford, go west on US 180 (Bankhead Highway) and follow it to TX 16. Turn south on TX 16 to Strawn, then turn east on FM 108, past Mingus, to Thurber.

*Some history:* Thurber can be considered a premier Texas ghost town, mainly due to its fascinating history as the only company-owned town that was also completely union-controlled in the state's history. In 1886, an engineer on the Texas and Pacific Railway discovered coal in the mountains surrounding Thurber in the 1880s. The Texas and Pacific Railway took over mining operations within two years, and founded the city of Thurber. Most of the people who lived in the town were coal miners from Mexico, France, England, Russia, Ireland, Italy, Poland, and Germany, plus a number

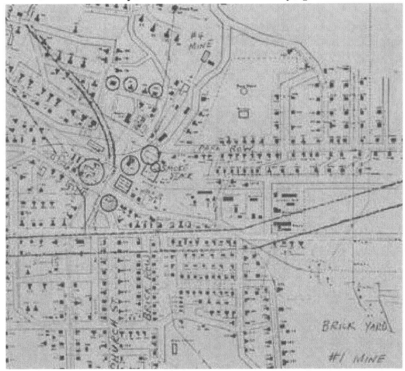

112.A 1960's map shows what Thurber used to look like with a population of 10,000 in 1920. The circles symbolize what buildings remained after the town closed (UT Arlington).

of other countries. Very soon, Americans and other immigrants moved to this new and exciting town to supply its inhabitants with groceries, entertainment, schooling, and more. However, the entire city was wholly owned by the Texas and Pacific Railway, including the houses, the library, the bank and of course, the mine. The company also began a secondary industry to supply pavers to towns and cities across the region. Access to the city was controlled by a barbed wire fence and armed guards to ward off undue unionization efforts, but that was for naught – all of the workers (miners, bartenders, brick makers, teachers, and more) organized under the United Mine Workers in 1903. The union and the company managed to strike a peaceful relationship for the next twenty years, when the Texas and Pacific Railway began investing in oil instead of coal – after all, oil field workers, whose work was sporadic, did not unionize. The miners and others left the town, and the mine itself was gated shut by the late 1920s. Thurber's descent into ghost town status was as quick as its ascent to a city.

*The sights*: Once you enter Thurber, you'll notice several bricked, sturdy buildings overgrown with vegetation, as well as the imposing coal mine's chimney. The brick manufacturing plant exists only as ground-level ruins. The tracks of the Texas and Pacific Railway's spur into the mining operations have been paved over but are still visible. Two restaurants — one inside the former ice house — are available for tourist dining. The ice house restaurant used to provide a key to Thurber's cemetery, and you'd have to leave your driver's license at the restaurant to retrieve the key. After the cemetery clean-up and restoration, this is no longer needed. Now, the cemetery can be visited on top of the hill with fantastic views of the country side. The cemetery features tombstones of deceased Polish, Mexican, French, German, and Czech residents. Additionally, the W.K. Gordon Center for Industrial History of Texas (operated by Tarleton State University) can be found in Thurber, where an extensive collection of Thurber ephemera and memorabilia is on display.

### By the way: The Bankhead Highway

113.The bricked alignment of the Bankhead Highway can be traversed west of Ranger, Eastland County.

The Bankhead Highway was once a National Auto Trail that connected Washington D.C. to San Diego (see page 98 for its route through the Red River Valley in Arkansas). Paved in the 1920s, it was named after John H. Bankhead, an Alabama Senator who was a great supporter of the project. In Texas, the Bankhead Highway enters the state as US 67 and, once in

Dallas, becomes US 80 to the west (the street has been re-numbered as US 180). Remains of the Bankhead Highway-including bridges, alignments, and abandoned gas stations - between Mineral Wells and Strawn can be visited.

### Fort Griffin Flat (Shackleford County)

*What's to see*: A fort in ruins at a state historic site, and the remains of the town at the base of the fort.

*How to get there*: From Thurber, travel back to Strawn. In Strawn, go south on TX 16 to the intersection with I-20, which goes west to Ranger. Take the first exit on the east side of Ranger, #354 – this is TX 254. Go west on TX 254 into Ranger and follow it to the west side of Ranger. On the west side is the very first alignment of the Bankhead Highway, still paved with brick. Go back onto I-20 west to Cisco, home of Conrad Hilton, who opened his first hotel here in 1919. From Cisco, travel north on TX 6 to Albany, thence north on US 283 to Fort Griffin.

Fort Griffin is a wonderful state historic site with plenty of ruins to visit, and Fort Griffin Flat, the town that accompanied the military fort, is located along the street at the northern base of Fort Griffin's hill. To get to The Flat, follow the dirt road to CR 188 (first dirt road on the northern side). Continue down this road to the ruins of the old town's 1870's truss bridge over the Brazos River, which is no longer passable but plenty scenic.

*Some history*: Prior to the Civil War, Camp Cooper served this area to protect settlers and travelers from hostile tribes. Both Robert E. Lee and William Tecumseh Sherman were stationed there. During the war, the U.S. closed down the camp because it was in the Confederacy. In 1867, after confederate defeat, the United States established Fort Griffin to continue securing the area. Soldiers stationed at the fort escorted wagon trains, stagecoaches, buffalo hunters, and surveying parties through this "hostile territory" – and sure enough, hostility reared its head. In 1871, a large group of Arapahoes, Cheyennes, Comanches, and Kiowas, who had left their reservation at Fort Sill, attacked teamsters employed by the Warren freighting company, who were ferrying supplies between Fort Richardson and Fort Griffin. Several of the teamsters men were killed. William Tecumseh Sherman, at this point Commander General of the U.S. Army, happened to be visiting Fort Richardson at this time to ascertain the Indian threat. He had traveled the same road just the day before the attack, but the Indians had spared him and his party. Sherman, realizing the danger, changed Indian policy right away: he declared an immediate military action against the southern Plains Indians to ensure they would never leave their reservations again. This strategy included the tactic of killing off the bison to discourage hunting. By 1875, the southern Plains Indian tribes were defeated in the Red River Wars. Fort Griffin lost its reason for being and closed in 1881.

During its brief life as a military post, hundreds of civilians moved to Fort Griffin to supply it with both needed provisions and dubious fun. They established a tent city at the base of the hill that grew into a fairly large town, which once counted almost 3,000 people. Sitting at the base of Fort Griffin's mesa, the town earned its name, "The Flat." Card sharps and wanton women plied their trades alongside saloon keepers, butchers, hide traders, and haberdashers. Cattle drovers on the Great Western Trail came through The Flat, adding to the plethora of people — including Doc Holliday, Big Nose Kate, Pat Garrett, Wyatt Earp, and John Wesley Hardin — who made this a rather lively, if lawless city. A few times, fort commanders had to declare martial law on The Flat to restore order. Eventually, the town's reputation aided in its own demise, as cowboys preferred the calmer atmosphere of nearby Albany. Then, the fort closed and the railroad bypassed the area completely. By the early twentieth century, Fort Griffin Flat was a goner.

*114.Calaboose at Fort Griffin Flat.*

*The sights*: Fort Griffin's ruins are very scenic, and an interpretive museum at the park headquarters will be well worth your time. Part of the Texas State Longhorn Herd gathers on-site to commemorate the fort's history along the Great Western Trail. The Flat has a number of buildings remaining that reflect its history, including a calaboose that, at last check, had a cactus growing on top. The bridge over the Brazos River, built in the 1870s, sits at the end of the road.

### By the way: The Suspension Bridge

In dry weather, a trip to Fort Griffin Flat can be even more adventurous with a visit to a historic suspension bridge. Bridges like this were once ubiquitous in Texas but are now seldom seen. From Fort Griffin, drive south on US 283 until the intersection with CR 179. Turn east and follow the road to the suspension bridge. William Flinn of the Flinn and Moyer Company built it around 1896. He camped near the site with his crew. The bridge once was the only local road to Fort Griffin. Today, the suspension bridge is no longer drivable, as a simple concrete bridge has replaced it. However, it is definitely walkable.

*115.A quite scenic place.*

### Not a Ghost, but Almost: Megargel (Archer County)

*What's to see*: An entire town.

*How to get there*: From Fort Griffin, follow US 283 north through Throckmorton (Throckmorton County seat). Then, on the north side of Throckmorton, take TX 79 northeast to Olney (Young County), where you will turn west on TX 114. Megargel is about 15 miles northwest of Olney on TX 114.

*Some history*: Megargel's ghost town status is debatable. The town began in 1910 on speculation by the Gulf, Texas and Western Railroad and was named after the railroad's president, Roy Megargel. The railroad's town building arm,

*116.One of several abandoned gas stations in Megargel.*

the Trinity Townsite Company, platted Megargel, which grew substantially in a very short amount of town because the investors offered buyers a discount to develop their lots. Oil discoveries led to a major boom. However, the Great Depression of 1929 hit the town hard. By the 1940s, the railroad — by then the Chicago, Rock Island and Pacific Railroad — stopped running. Many of the town's residents left to find work elsewhere. The population shrunk drastically, but the infrastructure could not, and much of what makes a town livable still abounds, including a park and a convenient store. However, Megargel's schools closed in 2006. The oil drilling operation that runs out of several downtown buildings hires some locals, but much of the work is feast-or-famine. Residents try to entice businesses and encourage ideas to keep the town from becoming completely abandoned, but it's an uphill battle.

*The sights*: Downtown Megargel has plenty of abandoned buildings, including many service stations that no longer serve anyone. The grain silos and corn mills stand as silent sentinels to the town's past. The 1927 high school is now privately owned. When I visited at mid-day, a skunk leisurely walked down the street.

### Mankins (Archer County)

*What's to see*: An old store and an abandoned, road side motel.

*How to get there*: From Megargel, go north/ northeast on FM 210 to Archer City. Archer City, the county seat of Archer County, has a fantastic museum located inside its restored jail. Although the museum is only open sporadically, the outside displays alone are well worth the visit. Also, Archer City is home to famed author Larry McMurtry's bookstore. At Archer City, turn north on TX SH 25 to its intersection with US 82. Mankins is located on this intersection.

*Some history*: Mankins, named after a ranch foreman of the Sam Lazarus ranch, developed along the Wichita Valley Railway in the late nineteenth century. In the early twentieth century, a brief oil boom enlivened the town, but not by much. It never recovered from a tornado that blew through in the late 1930s, and today, very few people live in Mankins.

*The sights*: A pretty church building, some disused buildings and a stone-covered tourist court are the only reminders of Mankins. US 82 used to bisect the town; now, the state has moved the highway behind Mankins atop the abandoned railroad tracks.

## Dundee (Archer County)

*What's to see*: An old school and a strip of a disused downtown.
*How to get there*: From Mankins, drive west on US 82 into Dundee.

*117.What's left of downtown Dundee.*

*Some history*: Dundee used to be the largest city in Archer County. It began its life as a ranch town that serviced the T Fork Ranch in the late nineteenth century. The Wichita Valley Railway came through, built a hotel and a station, and named the whole thing after a town in Scotland. Thus, Dundee was born and soon developed into a trading center for this portion of Archer County, with a bank, Masonic lodge, and other fine accoutrements. Unfortunately,

Dundee's existence didn't last long. A tornado in 1929, coupled with the dust bowl, hurt the town badly. Although the train came through until the late 1980s, it ceased servicing Dundee.

*The sights*: Now, the town is remembered by a string of brick store fronts along US 82 and a yellow-bricked school behind Main Street.

*118. Abandoned gas station in Dundee. Word to fellow road trippers: gas up before visiting these places!*

### Thrift (Wichita County)

*What's to see*: Remains of an oil boom. Or, technically, you'll be seeing the aftermath of an oil bust.

*How to get there*: From Wichita Falls (east of Dundee on US 82), go north to Burkburnett on either TX 240/ Burkburnett Road or Interstate 44. Pass through downtown Burkburnett using TX 240/ West 3rd Street. Turn north on Vaughn Road, then turn west onto Thrift Road. Thrift Road is a few miles long, ending at Morgan Road.

*Some history*: America's involvement in the Great War (1917-1919) convinced the military that in order to succeed in a globalizing economy, the U.S. needed oil, and lots of it. Luckily, Texas responded to this demand by way of its

*119.Trees of oil derricks in 1919 at Thrift, by Homer Hardin (LOC).*

geology. Until the 1940s, an oil boom blanketed many parts of Texas, and one of the largest and wildest was west of Burkburnett. Thousands of oil derricks sprouted from the Red River soil, and tens of thousands of workers descended onto the oil fields to take advantage of employment and business opportunities. The workers lived and worked in

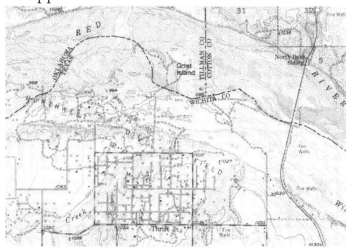

*120.Thrift on a topographical map from 1958 (USGS).*

tents, but Thrift, originally known as Newtown, built more permanent structures, with a brick bank building, post office, and school. Booms go bust, and this happened to Thrift. Although the little community hung around until the late 1950s, soil pollution from the oil fields, coupled with population loss, made Thrift a town that has gone with the wind.

*121.No more money in this bank in what was once the very wealthy town of Thrift in Wichita County.*

*The sights*: An abandoned brick building, which was once a bank, greets you at the intersection of Vaughn and Thrift Roads. Drive west on Thrift Road to see left over debris from the oil boom, especially as you pass over Wildhorse Creek on either Thrift, Bohner, or Morgan roads.

### Doan's Crossing (Wilbarger County)

*What's to see*: A cattle-drive era store.

*How to get there*: Drive to Vernon on US 287. From Vernon, go north on US 283 towards the Red River, then turn east on FM 2916. Doan's Crossing is at the end of FM 2916.

*Some history*: Not many settlements in the western portion of the Red River that date to the period before the railroads entered the area still exist in their "native state," but Doan's Crossing, established in 1878, does. The settlement grew around Jonathan Doan's trading post to serve drovers on the Great Western Trail, which stretched from the Texas hill country to Dodge City, Kansas. The trading post was also a

122.*In 1978, the Texas Historical Commission documented the historic adobe construction of the old Doan's store. Today, the store has been stuccoed to preserve the adobe beneath.*

beacon in this isolated stretch of Texas, as many people who were in route to settle Texas bought supplies and sent mail from here. When the cattle drives diminished due to increased fencing and farming, Doan's Crossing was supposed to be the starting point of a proposed national cattle road. The national cattle road would have been a large highway, unencumbered by barbed wire, that ensured that cattle driving would not become simply a rich man's business. Sadly, the proposal failed to pass the US senate. By the late nineteenth century, the railroad bypassed the town, and very soon, Doan's Crossing — once the most important settlement in northwestern Texas — was no more.

*The sights*: The original trading post, well-preserved by consistent maintenance efforts, still stands alongside a plethora of historical markers that indicate the importance of Doan's Crossing.

### By the way: The Red River Valley Museum

Vernon is home to the excellent Red River Valley Museum, located on the Vernon College campus. Exhibits include information on the Waggoner Ranch, one of the largest in the United States; the Great Western Trail; regional geology and weather; Comanches and pioneers; and other interesting tidbits of history about this portion of the Red River.

### Odell (Wilbarger County)

*What's to see*: A school, a calaboose, and lots of fields.

*How to get there*: From either Doan's Crossing or Vernon, go north on US 287 to FM 91. Turn west on FM 91 and follow it to Odell.

*Some history*: The Kansas City, Mexico and Orient Railway — simply known as the Texas Orient — established Odell in 1908, which grew into a large trading and farming center. Odell's decline started with several fires in the 1930s. The Atchison, Topeka and Santa Fe Railway acquired the Texas Orient line but pulled up all of the tracks in the late 1970s, marking the end of Odell.

*The sights*: While a post office still exists, the main traffic in Odell stems from farmers driving to their fields on their tractors. Remains of the town include the former jail, sitting in a field off Cooper Street, and an impressive stone-faced school that was built in the1920s. The former cotton gin is now a private residence.

The earliest residents of Odell came from Haulk, a town established in 1907 but bypassed by the railroad. The remains of Haulk are on private property but can be viewed on CR 103N off FM 91 between Odell and US 83.

*123.The calaboose, where the bad folks spent the night in Odell.*

### Thalia (Foard County)

*What's to see*: The high school, Masonic lodge, churches, and a desolate downtown.

*How to get there*: Return to Vernon. In Vernon, go west on US 287 for a short while, then take US 70 south for about 22 miles to Thalia.

*Some history*: Thalia is still a farming community but was once much bigger: it had an impressive high school, a vibrant downtown, a Masonic Lodge, and several churches that served its population. Founded around 1890, its hey-day was during the 1920's oil boom. By the 2000s, most of the town's businesses had fallen into ruins. Though Thalia doesn't have a movie theater, it was nonetheless the setting for novelist Larry McMurtry's *The Last Picture Show*.

According to the story, lots of things happen in Thalia, including prostitution and extra-marital affairs. Thalia is actually quite a bit tamer than this, with its citizens working to commemorate Thalia with art and events.

The *sights*: Half of Thalia's downtown (off US 70 on the north side) is in ruin; the other half is gradually being turned into a roadside park. The Masonic Lodge still stands, but hasn't seen much activity in years. The stone-faced Methodist Church sits lonely along a neighborhood street. The 1924 high school and its gym occupy the southern part of the town.

*124.A forlorn church in Thalia.*

### Medicine Mound (Hardeman County)

*What's to see*: Two beautiful buildings made from local stone and the ruins of a school.

*How to get there*: From Thalia, drive west on US 70 to Crowell, then turn north on TX 6. Turn east onto FM 1167 and follow the road to Medicine Mound, which sits off of a spur of FM 91. As you drive on FM 1167, you'll notice four mountains rising from the prairie, each taller than the other ones. These are the "Medicine Mounds," which served as sites for vision quests taken by the Comanches when this area was part of their territory.

*Some history*: Named for the Medicine Mounds, this little hamlet first saw life when the Kansas City, Mexico and Orient Railway platted it in 1908. Like the surrounding communities, its boom period was in the 1920s. A fire in the 1930s, possibly set by the spurned mistress of a nearby rancher, devastated the town, and the few buildings that were resurrected were constructed with round stones called "cannonballs" native to the Wichita Mountains in southwestern Oklahoma. Alas, it was all for naught — today, Medicine Mound is completely abandoned.

*125.Medicine Mounds' famous ruins were built from local materials.*

*The sights*: The general store and a large gas station, both now derelict, stand on either side of the town's Main Street. If you go further down Main Street, you'll pass over the old bed of the Kansas City, Mexico and Orient Railway. Beyond that, you will find the remains of Medicine Mound's school. The town's depot was moved to nearby Quanah and serves as a restaurant (as of this writing) on US 287 east of town.

126.*Medicine Mounds' former school with a thunderhead in the background.*

## By the way: Cynthia Ann and Quanah Parker

Near Medicine Mound is Copper Breaks State Park. To get there, take TX 6 south of Quanah. This park sits along the Pease River, which is the site where Cynthia Ann Parker, mother of famed Comanche chief Quanah, was re-captured by Texas Rangers in 1860. Her incredible story began when she was kidnapped by Comanches during a raid on her family's private fort in Limestone County in 1836. She was adopted by a Comanche woman and grew up as a member of the tribe. Cynthia then married Chief Peta Nokona, with whom she had several children, and lived happily as a Comanche until her husband was killed during the Battle of Pease River and the white participants recognized her as a kidnapped white woman. While the Texans considered her "saved" and were astonished by her story, Cynthia grew despondent. As a sign of deep mourning in the Comanche tradition, she cut her hair. She never saw her son, Quanah, again. Her daughter, Topsannah, died within a year of living with the whites, and Cynthia died soon thereafter. Along with her son and daughter, she is buried at the Fort Sill cemetery in Lawton, Oklahoma.

### Goodlett (Hardeman County)

*What's to see*: A store.

*How to get there*: Take FM 1167 west, then north to US 287 and follow US 287 west, past Quanah, to Goodlett.

*Some history*: Goodlett began as a ranching headquarters, then became a town when the Fort Worth and Denver Railway came through in 1889. Never a big place, it diminished with the loss of its school and the railroad.

127.*Lone remain of downtown Goodlett.*

*The sights*: Tucked away behind some brush is the old Goodlett store, each year getting the worse for wear. The school's gymnasium sits at the exit of the town.

## By the way: Chilicothe

I recommend taking a detour to Chillicothe, then continuing west on US 287. To get to Chillicothe, travel east and north on FM 91. A little depot of the Kansas City, Mexico and Orient Railway, later converted for the Santa Fe Railroad, sits in its original location off South 3rd Street. Also, Chillicothe's calaboose is on FM 91 on the north side of US 287, right next to an abandoned bank vault, and who wants to miss that? Quanah is also worth a visit. North of US 287 is its downtown, with an astonishingly beautiful depot and 1890's jail house anchoring a museum. Goodlett sits west of Quanah on the north side of US 287.

## Dodson (Collingsworth County)

*What's to see*: A tidy downtown – not really ghostly, but getting there.

*How to get there*: From Goodlett, take FM 680 (the next paved road west of town) all the way north to the bridge over the Prairie Dog Town Fork of the Red River. Once you cross the bridge, you're in Oklahoma. Keep going north until you reach US 62, then turn west to head back into Texas. Please note that the final portion of the road on the south side of the river is unpaved, so driving it is not recommended during wet weather. As an alternate route, keep traveling US 287 from Goodlet to Childress. In Childress, follow US 83 north US 62, then take US 62 east towards the Oklahoma border. Turn north on FM 1642 and follow it to Dodson.

*Some history*: Dodson began life as Dodsonville in the early twentieth century. It is still a fairly large town, but the loss of its school in the 1970s — due to consolidation with other schools in both Texas and Oklahoma — leads it into ghost town territory, though not quite. The cooperative cotton gin still brings farmers from around the area to downtown Dodson.

*The sights*: Downtown Dodson is pin-neat, but nearly abandoned, save for the cotton gin and its office.

### By the way: Randolph B. Marcy

Until recently, the bridge over the Prairie Dog Town Fork of the Red River along the road between Goodlett and Dodson was a one-lane, rickety wooden affair, but it's been replaced by a sterile concrete structure. The "Prairie Dog Town Fork" of the Red River got its name from Randolph B. Marcy, who was tasked in 1852 with discovering the headwaters of the Red River. He came upon thousands of prairie dog hills along this tributary, estimating that they housed over 20 million animals.

### Carey (Childress County)

128.In 1940, Dorothea Lange photographed Carey for the Farm Security Administration to help explain the effects of the Dust Bowl and New Deal programs on farming communities in the Great Plains (LOC).

*What's to see*: Stores and a school.

*How to get there*: From Dodson, drive northwest on FM 338 to Wellington, the county seat of Collingsworth County. In Wellington, turn south onto US 83 to get to Childress (Childress County seat). In Childress, turn west onto US 287. Carey is north of Childress along US 287. To get to Carey, you will need to briefly travel west on FM 328. Wellington is an important Bonnie and Clyde site, as described in *Traveling History with Bonnie and Clyde*.

129.What's left of Carey on the wind-swept prairie (yes, the rhyme was intentional).

*Some history*: Carey is a typical Texas panhandle town, owing its modern existence to the railroad. It began a little earlier, however. It was first named Talulah in honor of the teacher who worked in the first school in the late nineteenth century. The Fort Worth and Denver City Railway renamed the town. Once its cotton gin and school closed, and US 287 was re-routed to the east, Carey diminished.

*The sights*: A series of store fronts grace the original alignment of US 287. The brick school is hidden behind brush on a dirt road beyond the railroad tracks, across from the stores.

## Newlin (Hall County)

*What's to see*: A ghostly drug store.

*How to get there*: Newlin lies north of Estelline off US 287. Take FM 1619 west to Newlin.

*130. History stands in farmer's field in Newlin.*

*Some history*: The Texas panhandle was home to the Comanches as well as immense buffalo herds in the latter part of the nineteenth century. The Texas Rangers helped to clear out both, and many of the men who did this were awarded land in the former Comancheria. Charles Goodnight, for example, received over two thousand acres of land that centered on Palo Duro Canyon, which is a state park today. Fellow Ranger Andrew M. Embry also received a huge tract, on which the town of Newlin was built after the Fort Worth and Denver City Railway crossed the Prairie Dog

Town Fork of the Red River in 1889. The town grew into a sizeable settlement by the 1920s, but by the 1940s, the Dust Bowl and the Great Depression took their tolls. Today, Newlin has less than fifty people.

*The sights*: Newlin's former status as a town can only be witnessed by the remaining drug store, which sits behind a barbed wire fence.

This is the end of Texas's Red River Valley Ghost Town Tour!

Texas's share of ghost towns is just like its size — immense and varied. The remains of the former enclaves reflect the geographic diversity of the state, though not necessarily a historic diversity, as all of the settlements are of Anglo origin. To conclude the Texan share of the Red River Valley ghost town excursion, I recommend capping off with visits to two state parks: Caprock Canyons (near Quitaque) and Palo Duro Canyon (near Canyon).

### Caprock Canyons State Park

*How to get there*: From Estelline on US 287, go west on TX 86 through Turkey and then on to Quitaque. Once in Quitaque, turn north onto FM 1065 and follow it to the park.

*What is it?* The caprock is a geological formation that denotes where the prairies break apart as the upswelling of the Llano Estacado (Staked Plains) begins. This narrow but long sliver of geology features red clay, limestone, mica, and other loose rocks and soil that has hardened and weathered through millions of years in the drought/flood cycles of this region.

*Some history:* Caprock Canyons State Park occupies land that was in the territories of the Kiowa, Comanche, and Apache tribes, who camped along the Little Red River and its tributaries. It was also an area of trade between Native American tribes and New Spain, as roads to Santa Fe and Chihuahua crossed here. In the 1870s, Charles Goodnight and John Adair set up huge ranches along the caprock, which were served by railroads that came through in the early twentieth century. Mid-century, the state of Texas acquired the ranch land through donations and sales and by 1975, it opened the park to house a historic remnant of the original plains buffalo. This herd has grown into several hundred animals. The railroad bed now serves as a sixty-two mile trail that links Quitaque and Silverton.

*131.Clarity Tunnel along the trail at Caprock Canyon.*

*What's to do?* Along the Caprock Canyon State Park Trail is the Clarity Tunnel, the only railroad tunnel in Texas that can be traversed. Bats roost here all year long. Other wildlife is also prominent in the park, as it hosts the official Texas State Bison Herd. Normally, the bison just stand around, chewing or braying. You can also hike around the canyon on trails or along the dry creek beds. The creeks are prone to flash floods in wet weather.

## Palo Duro Canyon State Park

*How to get there*: From Estelline on US 287, go west on TX 86 past Turkey, Quitaque, and Silverton to Tulia. In Tulia, turn north on US 87/ I 27 and follow it to Canyon. In Canyon, go east on FM 217/ 4th Avenue to Palo Duro Canyon State Park.

*What is it?* Palo Duro Canyon is an immense outcropping of the caprock that developed at the sources of the Red River. It is one of the largest canyons in the United States, second in size only to the Grand Canyon. The Prairie Dog Town Fork of the Red River runs through the canyon as it flows from its spring-fed source near Canyon, Texas.

*Some history*: Evidence of habitation in Palo Duro Canyon can be seen by stone-age rock art, produced over ten thousand years ago. By the seventeenth century, the canyon was well known to the Comanches, Kiowas, and Apaches as a good camping spot as they followed the bison herds, and the Spanish made note of the canyon on their maps. However, Spanish colonial settlement was not successful due to the Comanches' claims on the land. After the Louisiana Purchase in 1803, the Jeffersonian government attempted to accurately map the source of the Red River. This feat was finally accomplished in 1852. Randolph B. Marcy and George B. McClellan took a contingent of troops from Preston in Grayson County (see page 185) up the Red

River along the Chihuahua Trail and then, the old Spanish Road in western Oklahoma. They mapped the sources for the Red and Canadian rivers as they came upon Palo Duro Canyon. They determined that the area would be conducive to American settlement once the Comanches were out of the way. This happened in 1875. The Red River Wars, fought between American soldiers and bands of the southern Plains Indians beginning in 1874, emptied the caprock of the Comanches and other tribes, who were forced to live on their reservation at Fort Sill in Indian Territory. The last of the Red River War battles was fought inside Palo Duro Canyon.

132.*Absolute beauty at the birthplace of the Red River: Palo Duro Canyon.*

Charles Goodnight, a cattle drover who blazed the Goodnight-Loving Trail, began a ranching operation in the 1870s along the caprock. He was backed by money from John Adair, a Colorado business man, whose million-acre holdings encompassed Palo Duro Canyon. The Goodnight and Adair ranches did not just maintain cattle, though. The canyons were also home to the last remnant of the Southern bison herd. Charles Goodnight's wife Mary convinced him to save the bison for future generations; her advice helped to establish the heritage herd now at home in Caprock Canyon State Park.

Texas bought Goodnight's portion of the ranch land in the 1930s, and the Civilian Conservation Corps began building structures and expanding paths to make the canyon into a state park.

*What's to do?* Beyond hiking, biking, and camping amid the majestic red rocks, Palo Duro Canyon plays host to several star-gazing events, photography workshops, and full-moon hikes. Each summer, the state park stages the musical *Texas* outside in the amphitheater.

## End of the Road

The death of towns is no laughing matter. The families who lived there, the businesses that served them, and the landscapes that made up their homes all had stories to tell. The point of ghost town hunting is to find these stories through the remains left behind. And, as the lure of the cities siphon the workforce, schools whither from lack of students and funding, and old-time beliefs and traditions fade with the past generations, ghost towns will continue to populate a region that has always been based on the ability for people to be mobile.

Seek out these places that we call "ghost towns" and revel in their haunting beauty. Take photographs, leave only foot prints. Talk to the clerk at the lone gas station still open in town. Even better, see if there's an old-timer mowing the grass who'd love a short visit. Walk down the streets, or what's left of them, and ignore the barking dog that, inevitably, will follow you. Drive slowly, roll down the window, and enjoy the breeze as you travel into the past.

## Happy Trails!

# *Resources*

*Pertinent museums and parks up the Red River, arranged by tour.*

## LOUISIANA MUSEUMS AND PARKS

Louisiana History Museum
- 503 Washington Street, Alexandria, LA 71301. 318-487-8556.
- Special and permanent exhibits focus on the big themes of Louisiana history, including its rather complicated political past. Space is devoted to Civil War history, commerce, household items, and other artifacts.

Solomon Northrup Trail
- An eighty-three-mile trip through sites between Marksville and Alexandria takes travelers where Solomon Northrup, who wrote the slave narrative *Twelve Years a Slave*, endured human trafficking. Download the map to learn what remains can still be seen.

Marksville State Historic Site
- 837 Martin Luther King Drive, Marksville, LA 71351
- Call 318-484-2390 to schedule a site visit.
- Prehistoric ceremonial center with burial mounds from relatives of the Hopewell culture sit next to an ancient remnant of the Red River's waterway.

Forts Randolph and Buhlow and State Historic Site
- 135 Riverfront Street, Pineville, LA 71360. 318-484-2390
- After the violence endured during Union occupation from 1863 to 1864, the Confederate state built earthenwork forts at the rapids in the Red River by

Alexandria to protect from further incursions. The Civil War was over by 1865, however, so the forts were never used. Their structures are returning to nature but can still be viewed along pretty walking paths.

Cane River Creole National Historical Park
- 400 Rapides Drive, Natchitoches, LA 71457. 318-352-0383 x.316
- The National Park System preserves two plantations and the stories of the people who lived along the Red and Cane rivers. The bayous and meandering waterways south of the Great Raft helped to create an insular community that centered on a handful of French and Creole families. Their descendants still speak French Creole and actively participate in historic, church, and community engagements — in other words, the whole complex is a living museum.

Fort St. Jean Baptiste State Historic Site
- 155 Jefferson Street, Natchitoches, LA 71457. 318-357-3101.
- This recreated fort sits on the original location of the Natchitoches tribe's village, which was subsumed to become a French trading post and ultimately, the historic city of Natchitoches.

Los Adaes State Historic Site
- 6354 Highway 485, Robeline, LA 71449.
- In 1716, the Spanish founded a mission and presidio amid the Adaen people to assert their claims to lands west of the Red River. When the French Fort St. Jean Baptiste gained in trading prominence, Los Adaes even became the governmental seat of colonial Texas until the Spanish took over Louisiana Territory in

1763. The mission and fort are long gone, but the Camino de Real (Spanish road that linked Natchitoches to Mexico) can be well ascertained inside the archeological site.

Fort Jesup State Historic Site
- 32 Geoghagan Road, Many, LA 71449
- Established in 1822, this fort protected the U.S. and Mexico border when nearby Texas was still under Mexican control. American volunteers in the Texas Revolution (1836) and in the Mexican-American War (1846-1848) mustered here. Abandoned by the federal government in 1869, the fort's stone buildings and foundations can be visited.

Grand Ecore Visitors Center
- 106 Tauzin Island Road, Natchitoches, LA 71457. 318-354-8770.
- The Visitor Center offers beautiful views of the high bluff on the north side of Natchitoches, as well as a fantastic facility with educational displays about the Red River and the Army Corps of Engineers role in maintaining flood control and navigation.

Campti Historical Museum
- 211 Edenborn Street, Campti, LA 71411. 318-476-2990.
- Located inside a former bank building, the museum reflects the historic diversity of Campti and the surrounding areas with artist workshops, cultural events, quilting bees, and special exhibits. The museum is also home to a working farm with the innovative model of "community supported agriculture." Locals can rent a block of garden to harvest their own herbs and vegetables.

Red River Crossroads Historical and Cultural Association
- 12797 Main Street, Gilliam, LA 71029. 318-296-4303.
- While only open sporadically, this museum offers insight into northwestern Louisiana after the Civil War, when oil discoveries created a population boom amid cotton plantations and racial violence.

## ARKANSAS ARCHIVES AND PARKS

Historic Washington State Park
- 103 Franklin Street, Washington, AR 71862. 870-983-2684.
- The whole town of Washington, once the seat of Hempstead County until Hope got the nod in the early twentieth century, can be considered a ghost town — but it's wonderfully preserved in this historic park that merits a day's worth of exploration.

SARA – Southwestern Arkansas Regional Archives
- 201 AR 195, Washington, AR 71862. 870-983-2633.
- This is a great research stop for anyone interested in the history along the Great Bend of the Red River. There's a lot of information for genealogists as well as people interested in maps and overall history.

## OKLAHOMA MUSEUM AND PARKS

Museum of the Red River
- 812 East Lincoln Road, Idabel, OK 74745. 580-286-3616
- A state-of-the-art, archeological repository for artifacts pertaining to the indigenous people of the Red River Valley, this amazing facility holds countless Native American artifacts, from pottery to cradles to baskets to clothes.

Wheelock Academy Historic Site
- US 70 in Millerton, OK. 580-746-2139.
- The academy for Choctaw girls, which opened in 1832, is the only extant one in the Red River Valley of several educational institutions built by and for the Chickasaw and Choctaw tribes that has been preserved as a historic site. Several wooden buildings from the 1870s and 1880s explain the institution; the cemetery demonstrates the troubles in this new land; and the Presbyterian Church, the oldest stone structure in Oklahoma, attests to the site's endurance.

Fort Towson Historic Site
- HC 63, Box 1580, Fort Towson, OK 74735. 580-873-2634.
- The site contains the ruins of the 1824 fort built to maintain peace between Americans, the Choctaws and Chickasaws, and indigenous people along the Red River.

Boggy Depot State Park
- 475 Park Drive, Atoka, OK 74525. 580-889-5625
- This park is the former site of Boggy Depot, one of Oklahoma's premier ghost towns. While no structures remain, the cemetery's tombstones are worth an extended visit.

Fort Washita Historic Site
- 3348 OK 199, Durant, OK 74701. 580-924-6502.
- The original stone structures remain of this 1842 fort built to protect the Chickasaws and Choctaws from attacks by the Comanches and Kiowas. The fort also served as a staging area for the Mexican American War (1846-1848). The ruts of the military road are still readily visible within the site.

Atoka County Museum and Civil War Cemetery
- 2902 North Highway 69, Atoka, OK 74525. 580-889-7192.
- The museum's grounds hold the most interest for a ghost town hunter, as the Texas Trail (Shawnee Trail) is visible. The cemetery contains a number of Confederate soldiers' graves from the 19th Arkansas Infantry who died from a measles outbreak.

Three Valley Museum
- 401 W. Main Street, Durant, OK 74701. 580-920-1907.
- The museum harks back to the early days of the areas and also salutes veterans and Purple Heart recipients through exhibits and events.

Old Greer County Museum
- 222 West Jefferson Street, Mangum, OK 73554. 580-782-2851.
- The museum showcases a number of artifacts from pioneer families and early settlers when the area was still claimed by Texas.

**TEXAS MUSEUMS AND PARKS**

Museum of Regional History
- 219 N. State Line Avenue, Texarkana, TX 75501. 903-793-4831.
- Lots of good prehistoric materials as well as nods to the surrounding area.

Enloe Museum
- 218 Lexie Street, Enloe, TX 75441. 903-784-8114.
- The museum commemorates the people and the town that once was larger than it is now.

Grayson County Frontier Village
- Loy Lake Park, 111 RC Vaughan Drive, Denison, TX 75021. 903-463-2487.
- Several pioneer cabins and historic homes, all moved to the site over the past fifty years, are open for viewing at the park. The park sits next to Loy Lake, a popular recreational site enjoyed by Grayson County residents.

Red River Railroad Museum
- 101 East Main Street, Denison, TX 75021. 903-463-5289.
- The small museum contains a lot of history about the many railroads that helped spur the economic growth in North Texas after the Civil War.

Tales 'n Trails Museum
- 1522 US 82, Nocona, TX 76255. 940-825-5330.
- Lots of history about the area is preserved and on display, but special attention should be paid to the artifacts from Spanish Fort, the famous ghost town along the Abilene Cattle Trail.

Fort Richardson State Park and Historic Site
- 228 Park Road 61, Jacksboro, TX 76458. 940-567-3506.
- This extensive site is not just an Indian-war era fort, but also provides much context history within its landscapes. The parade grounds are ringed by preserved buildings; the now-abandoned Great Texas and Western Railroad cuts a path just behind the fort and serves as part of a trail; the trail leads to Jacksboro Lake; and next to the trail are ruts of the Butterfield Overland Stagecoach line as well as the old baptismal pond. This is an excellent place to camp overnight or just hang out for a day.

Fort Belknap
- 5385 FM 61, Newcastle, TX 76372. 940-846-3222.
- The fort, which opened in 1852, was restored using WPA funds and is now operated by Young County. The cemetery is a very interesting frontier relic, as are the fort museum's collections.

W.K. Gordon Center for Industrial History of Texas
- 65258 I-20, Mingus, TX 76463. 254-968-1886.
- This highly interesting and modern museum celebrates the ghost town of Thurber, once the center of the coal mining industry in Texas.

Fort Griffin State Historic Site
- 1701 U.S. 283, Albany, TX 76430. 325-762-3592.
- The fort, built immediately after the Civil War, lies in ruins along a picturesque ridge. The visitor's center offers a plethora of artifacts from the site. At the base of the fort sits the ghost town of Fort Griffin Flat and its few but very interesting structures.

Red River Valley Museum
- 4600 College Drive, Vernon, TX 76384. 940-553-1848.
- The museum celebrates indigenous, settlement, and cattle trailing periods of northwestern Texas, with a special room dedicated to the Waggoner Ranch, the once-largest ranch in the United States.

# How-Tos

### How to prepare for a Ghost Town Hunt

Though not all of life needs to go according to plan, a bit of foresight will make for a successful ghost town hunting expedition by maximizing the areas to discover. Additionally, it is wise to plan your hunt according to season and weather conditions; although winter is the best time to see ruins that can be often obscured by vegetation, the winter light can mar photographs. Summer may have the best daylight, but it can also be a buggy, miserably hot time of year.

Bugs do not create the only problems. Every ghost town hunter should bring insect repellant and sunblock, wear sturdy shoes, and take a walking stick to probe the ground for potential hidden dangers, like snakes, holes, and rivers of sewage (yes, that's happened before).

Of course, ghost town hunters should bring a camera and perhaps a notebook to jot down information and even make sketches. Taking a bit of food and drink is a wise choice. All road trippers must ensure that vehicles are in good condition. It's recommended to carry insurance that includes towing coverage.

All historical ghost town hunters also know that the only items to take from a ghost town are photographs. If you find something that is out of the ordinary or you believe it is of historical value, make sure to contact the historical commission or society for the appropriate state. Note the location and date of discovery. As always, trespassing should be highly discouraged, as it is a crime and is also quite dangerous.

## How to plan for a Ghost Town Hunt

Whenever you choose to go, the following two atlas series can help the explorer "read" the landscape.

DeLorme Atlases
- These detailed atlases are a must for trips that may take travelers beyond the range of a phone app.
- DeLorme Atlas Maps depict each road within each county of the respective state. Often, cemeteries and random buildings listed as "community centers" indicate the presence of a ghost town.
- These atlases are available at any book and outdoor/sports retailers.

SPV Atlases
- Many towns lived and died by the tracks of abandoned railroads; SPV atlases depict disused lines where these towns once thrived.
- The atlases are arranged by region. For the purposes of exploring the Red River Valley, this means that Louisiana, Arkansas, Oklahoma, and Texas are all located in different atlases and must be purchased separately.
- These atlases are usually available through online retailers or as special orders from your local bookstore.

Google Maps and/or Google Earth
- The ability of satellite images has been a boon for ghost-town hunters. Use the aerial maps before a hunt and perhaps save or print them, as often, cell phone coverage is spotty in these out-of-the-way places. Look for old schools & disused downtowns.
- Memorize or print Google Maps as auto-navigational tools often do not recognize ghost towns.

## How to research a Ghost Town

Gas money can be tight, so it makes sense to check out possible ghost towns on-line before making a trip to a place that is literally "gone with the wind." Certain websites help out in this capacity.

The Encyclopedia of Arkansas History and Culture
- www.encyclopediaofarkansas.net
- Encyclopedia-type entries about events, counties, towns, rivers, parks, people, railroads, and sundries, written by local, regional, and national historians, assist the intrepid explorer in understanding the history of places in Arkansas. However, primary sources are lacking – and lamentably, the Arkansas Gazette, the oldest newspaper west of the Mississippi still in publication, has not been digitized.

Oklahoma Historical Society
- www.okhistory.org
- This excellent website features newspapers, articles about historical topics, photographs, and encyclopedia entries on all things related to Oklahoma's fascinating history.

KNOWLA: The Digital Encyclopedia of Louisiana
- www.leh.org
- An ever-evolving and often frustrating website, the encyclopedia is difficult to access and most of the information from the Louisiana Endowment for the Humanities focuses on New Orleans.

64 Parishes
- www.64parishes.org/encyclopedia
- Although the landing page attempts to lure visitors into featured articles, the information contained is sound, although a bit too academic in its content.

Unlike Oklahoma's encyclopedia, this site does not offer access to primary sources.

State Library of Louisiana
- www.louisianadigitallibrary.org
- An excellent resource of old photographs, maps, and other digitized, primary source content.

Portal to Texas History
- https://texashistory.unt.edu
- While the search feature is a bit difficult to navigate, this collaborative effort between universities, museums, libraries, and historical societies has created a huge repository of photographs, newspapers, maps, and other primary source documents.

Handbook of Texas Online
- https://tshaonline.org
- There are thousands of well-researched and compact articles on everything, everyplace, and everyone related to Texas history. However, no primary sources are present.

David Rumsey Map Collection
- www.davidrumsey.com
- Many of these maps are for sale, but luckily, they are also searchable and zoomable. The Rumsey collection has maps and atlases that no one else in the world has, and the collection is continuously updated.

Library of Congress
- www.loc.gov
- "The LOC" has tens of thousands of photographs, maps, newspapers, government documents, books, recordings, historical collections – all related to the

history and culture of the United States. Searching is relatively easy, although the plethora of information can be a bit overwhelming.

Google Maps and Google Earth
- www.google.com/maps
- www.google.com/earth
- Both sites offer satellite images and GPS coordinates of all locations mentioned in this book and beyond. They are great tools to uncover potential ghost towns, especially when using the "street view" feature. While there are sites with "historic aerials" of certain towns and features, they are not recommended due to the cost in obtaining the images.

## *Sources used for this book*

Arkansas Historical Commission.
- Southwestern Arkansas Regional Archives
- Various maps

Dallas Public Library.
- The Territorial Papers of the United States, edited and compiled by Clarence Edwin Carter. Washington, D.C.: United States Government Printing Office, 1940.
  - The Territory of Arkansas, vols. 19, 20 and 21 (1819-1836)
  - The Territory of Orleans, vol. 9 (1803-1812)

DeGoyler Library at Southern Methodist University.
- Various ephemera

Federal Writer's Project.
- The Indian-Pioneer Papers (University of Oklahoma, Western History Collection)
- The Slave Narratives (Library of Congress, Born in Slavery Collection)
- Guides to the States (Louisiana, Arkansas, Oklahoma, and Texas).

Handbook of Texas On-line.
- Various entries

David Rumsey Map Collection.
- Various maps

Library of Congress.
- Chronicling America: Digitized Newspapers
- Various map collections

Northeast Texas Digital Archives.
- Various ephemera

Oklahoma Historical Society.
- Encyclopedia of Oklahoma
- Gateway to Oklahoma History

Perry Castaneda Library.
- Sanborn Fire Insurance Maps

Portal to Texas History.
- Digitized Texas Newspapers
- Various map collections
- Various Bird's Eye View maps

Red River Historian.
- Robin Cole-Jett, writer and publisher

SPV's Comprehensive Railroad Atlas of North America.
- Mike Walker (Stuart Andrews, Publisher for SPV, Kent, UK)
    - Prairies East and Ozarks (2004)
    - Prairies West (2002)
    - Southern States (2001)
    - Texas (2001)

# *Index*

Aaron School (OK) 4,5,114,158
Abilene Cattle Trail/McCoy Trail/Chisholm Trail 43,43i,146,147,148, 150,194,246
Adair, John 237
Adams-Onis Treaty, 30
Addington (OK) 3,7i,114,146,147-148,150
Alexandria 5i,27,40,44,50,54,55,58,59,61,240,241,
All-black towns 142,143
Alleene (AR) 3,87,110-111
Altus 147,154,155,157,158,159,
Altus, Wichita Falls and Hollis Railway 158
American Plantation Row 81
Amtrak 137
Anadarko (OK) 34
Antelope (TX) 4,170,202-203,204
Apaches 21,114,149,151,161,167,193,205,235,236
Arapahoes 139, 165,214
Arbuckle Mountains 135,136,137
Ardmore (OK) 135
Arthur City (TX) 4,8i,170,175-176
Armstrong Academy 33,122
Army Corps of Engineers 34,35,37,71,242
Ashdown (AR) 111,113
Atchison, Topeka and Santa Fe Railway 138, 224
Atoka Museum 128
Austin, Moses 30
Austin, Stephen 30,88,104

Bankhead Highway 6i,8i,47,48,97,98,209,212-213
Baton Rouge 55,58
Battle of Mansfield 75-76
Battle at Middle Boggy Depot 127
Battle of Pease River 228
Battle of Spanish Fort 21,192-196
Baylor, John 206
Bayou Boeuf 25,55,56,57
Bayou Pierre 55
Bayou Robert 55
Belcher (LA) 3,54,80-81
Belcherville (TX) 4,170,196-197
Ben Lomand (AR) 3,87,108,109
Bermuda/ Oakland Plantation (LA) 3,5i,54,65-67
Big Cypress Bayou/Creek 34,35
Bison 22,24,30,161,201,236,237,238

Black Diamond (AR) 89-90
Bloomfield Academy 33
Bog Monster 90
Boggy Depot (OK) 3,7i,32i,33,39,114,125-128,129,244
Bonham (TX) 179
Bonita (TX) 4,170,191
Boston (New, Old) (TX) 8i,19,30,173-174
Bowie Knife 58
Boyd, Billy 181
Boyd, Glory 181
Boyd Hill 88,94-95,
Brazos Indian Reservation 33,205
Brazos River 24,33,205,207,208,213,216
Broken Bow (OK) 116
Bromide (OK) 19,7i,47,114,131-134
Brookston (TX) 4,170,176-177,178
Buffalo Springs (TX) 4,8i,170,200-202
Butterfield Overland Mail and Stagecoach Company 36,127,128-129,134,246
Bureau of Indian Affairs 115
Burney Academy 33
Byars (OK) 3,7i,114,

Caddoan Mounds 19,80,81,88,240
Caddo Lake 33,34
Caddos (tribe) 18-20,28,29,33,67,69,70,73,80-81,87,89,94,100,119,123,175,206
Cairo and Fulton Railroad 91,96,101,104
Camino de Real 26,36,67,242
Camp Arbuckle 139
Camp (Fort) Cooper 40,213
Cane River 34,59,64,65,241
Cane River Creoles 64-65
Cane River Creole National Heritage Area 54,62,65,241,26
Cannon (TX) 4,36,170,180-181
"Cannonball" architecture 161,227
Caprock 24,167,172,234,235,236,237
Caprock Canyons 9i,234-236
Carey (TX) 4,9i,170,231-232
Cast Iron Forest 22
Caspiana (LA) 3,6i,54,71-72
Cheyennes 139,165,214
Chicago, Rock Island, and Pacific Railroad 145,147,149i,151,164,198,200,207,208
Chickasaws 32,33,88,112,115,119,123,126,139,141,185,244
Chickasaw Recreational Area/ Platt National Park 139-140
Chihuahua Trail 88,178,237

Chillicothe 230
Chisholm, Jesse 146
Chisholm Trail/McCoy Trail/Abilene Cattle Trail 43,43i,146,147,148, 150,194,246
Choctaws 17,31,33,88,100,112,115,117,118,119,122,123,141,185,244
Chopin, Kate 59
Civilian Conservation Corps 91,140,238
Civil War 30,31,38-42,43,44,55,56,61,66,67,68,72,74,75,77,85,91,96,100i,101, 108,120,122,127, 133,134,141,171,177,179,181,184,187,191,201,203, 205,206, 213,240,241,243,245,246,247
Clarita (OK) 3,114,130-131
Clarity Tunnel 9i,235,236
Cloud Chief (OK) 4,114,165
Cloutierville (LA) 3,5i,54,59-60,61
Coffee, Holland 38,146,185,186,193
Coincoin, Marie Therese Metoyer 26,63,64-65
Colbert (OK) 36,50
Colbert's Ferry 36
Columbus (AR) 3,87,105-106
Comanches 18,21-24,38,40,46,151,167,171,185,192,193,201,204,205,206, 214,224,226,228,233,236, 237,244
Comancheria 23,170,205,206,233
Comancheros 24,192
Cooperton (OK) 4,114,161,163
Cottonbelt/St. Louis and Southwestern Railway 92
Cross Timbers/Cast Iron Forest/Grand Prairie 14,22,24,33,139,175,
Custis & Freeman Expedition/Red River Expedition 27,28,29,94
Cut Finger 29,94

Dallas 11,36,37i,43,44,50,182,213,256-257
Dallas Public Library 253Dalton Gang 167
Davis, Jefferson 96
Dawes Act (1887) 46
de la Harpe, Bernard 20,145
Derry/ Magnolia Plantation (LA) 3,5i,54,60-62,
desegregation 42,143,160
de Soto, Hernando 19
Denison (TX) 44,50,187,245,246
Denison, Bonham and New Orleans Railroad 179
Denison Dam 186
Dexter (TX) 4,8i,45,170,187-188
Dixie Overland Highway 47
Doan's Crossing (TX) 4,9i,170,222-224
Doddridge (AR) 3,6i,87,89-90
Dodge City 167,223

Dodson (TX) 4,170,230-231,232
Dooley's Ferry 92
Dorchester (TX) 4,8i,183-184
Dougherty (OK) 3,7i,51,114,135-137,138-139,140
Dundee (TX) 4,5i,8i,170,219-220
Durant (OK) 124,125,126,244,245
Dust Bowl 49,155,159,220,231,234

Eisenhower, Dwight 50
Eliasville (TX) 4,8i,207-209,210
Elmer (OK) 4,114,155-156
English (TX) 4,30,170,172-173
Enloe (TX) 4,8i,170,178-179,245
Enloe Museum 179,245
Exoduster 142

Faxon (OK) 3,7i,114,150-151,152
Ferries 36
Fleetwood (OK) 3,114,145,146
Folsom, Israel 33,120
Fort Arbuckle 37,38
Fort Belknap 40,205-206,207,247,
Fort Griffin 213-216,247
Fort Griffin Flat 4,8i,41,170,213-216,247
Fort Richardson 204-205,214,246
Fort Sill 5i,24,25,145,151,215,229,237
Fort St. Jean Baptiste 20,241
Fort Supply 40
Fort Towson 3,33,35,100,104,117,121,122,123-124,125,244
Fort Washita 3,7i,39,133-134,244
Fort Worth and Denver City Railway 229,232,234
Fouke (AR) 90
Freedmen/freed people 26,31,41,42,55,57,61,62,64,101,107,141
French Louisiana 25i,26
Frontier Village 187,246
Fulton (AR) 3,6i,30,36,44,87,95-98,99,104,175
Fulton, Samuel 175

Gage Creek 208
Gainesville (TX) 39,45,187,188
Gainesville, Henrietta and Western Railway 189,191,196
Garland City (AR) 3,6i,36,87,92-94,95
Gene Autry (OK) 3,114,134-135
Gilliam (LA) 82
Gloster (LA) 3,54,72-73

Goodlett (TX) 4,9i,170,229,230,231
Goodland Academy 122
Goodland Academy 122
Gold Rush Road 126,139
Goodnight, Charles 205,233,235,237
Goodnight-Loving Trail 205,237
Goodnight, Mary 237
Gotebo (OK) 4,8i,42,114,163-165,166
Grand Ecore (LA) 3,28,54,67-68,76,242
Grand Ozages 29,94
Grand Prairie 22
Graysonia, Nashville, and Ashdown Railroad 107
Great Bend 20,47i,87,88,89,95,96,96i,97,243
Great Depression 48,49,71,144,147,159,177,178,202,217,234
Great Hanging at Gainesville 39
Great Red River Raft 28,33-35,68,70-71,81,84,241
Great War (World War I) 47,48,177,221
Greer County War 167
Guerrero (Coahuilia) 67
Gulf, Colorado and Santa Fe Railway 135,136
Gulf, Texas and Western Railroad 203,217

Hart, John 185
Haulk (TX) 225
Headrick (OK) 4,7i,114,153-155
Heartland Flyer 137
*Heliopolis* 34
Hersey, Tim 146
Hobby Highway 47,137
Hollister (OK) 4,7i,114,152-153,154
Honey Creek 137
Hope (AR) 45,91,101,103
Hopewell Culture 240
Hosston (LA) 3,6i,54,81-82
Houston and Texas Central Railroad 5i,44,45i,180
Humphreys (OK) 4,7i,114,156-157
Hunter, Clementine 63

Idabel (OK) 118,119,121,243
Ike Cloud Ranch 144
Illinois Bend (TX) 4,8i,170,189,191-192
Illinois Central Railroad 44
Irving, Washington 22

Jackson, Andrew 115,117

J. Bennett Johnston Waterway 69
Jean (TX) 4,8i,170,203-204,205
Jefferson (TX) 35,173
Jefferson Highway 47,68,79,124-125
Jefferson, Thomas 27,236
Jim Crow 142
Jonesboro (TX) 4,30,35,122,170,174-175
Joutel, Henri 19
Justin, H.J. 195

Kansas City Bridge Company 93
Kansas City, Mexico and Orient Railway 155,224,227,230
Kansas City Southern Railway 80,
Kansas, Oklahoma and Gulf Railroad (Missouri, Oklahoma and Gulf Railway)
130,132
Keachi aka Keatchi, Keatchie, Keechi (LA) 3,6i,54,73-75,76
Keechis 20
Kiowa-Comanche-Apache Reservation 151,161,149
Kiowas 46,151,162,163,167,192,204,214,236,244
King of Trails Highway 47,130
Ku Klux Klan 41

Lake Texoma 50,184,186
Lange, Dorothea 5,9,49,231,
Lattimore, Tim 148
Laynesport (AR) 35,113
Lee Highway 47,124-125
Lee, Robert 47,124,214
Lehigh (OK) 3,7i,114,129-130
Leon (OK) 3,7i,114,144,145
Little Red River 235
Little Rock 101,102,104,
Library of Congress 253
Llano Estacado 234
Logansport (LA) 30
Loggy Bayou 55
Lone Wolf v. Hitchcock (1903) 151-152
Los Adaes 18,67,241
Louisiana Purchase 27,29,52,88,236,
Louisiana Railway and Navigation Line 80,85,105
Loveland (OK) 3,114,152,153
Loving, Oliver 205
Lynching 41,83,171

Magnolia Plantation/Derry (LA) 3,5i,54,60-62,

Mankins (TX) 4,170,218-219
Mansfield (LA) 40,74,75,76
Marcy, Randolph 37,38,231,237
Marysville (TX) 4,8i,170,188-189
Mayers (LA) 3,6i,54,79-80
Masonic Hall or Lodge 73,75,77,86,90,101,103,169,220,225,226
McClellan, George 37,237
McCoy, Joseph 43,146
McCoy Trail/Chisholm Trail/Abilene Cattle Trail
43,43i,146,147,148,150,194,246
McKenzie, Ranald 205
McMurtry, Larry 218,225
Medicine Lodge Creek Treaty 46,204
Medicine Mounds (TX) 4,9i,170,226-228
Medicine Park (OK) 48
Meeker (LA) 3,19i,54,56-57,58,59-60
Megargel (TX) 4,8i,170,216-218
Meridian Highway 7i,47,148-150,200
Mexican American War 124,244
Mexican Texas 30,31,96,124,194i
Millwood Lake 107,108
Mineral Wells (TX) 48,132,209,213
Mira (LA) 3,6i,54,83-84
Missouri Compromise 29
Missouri-Kansas-Texas Railroad 44,127,171,179,187,189,190,191,198
Missouri River 27
Mississippi River 14,26,29,32,38,55,57,61,88,114,120,184
Monroe, James 117
Moseley, Joel 158
Moorehead/Rosalie Plantation (LA) 3,54,58-59
Museum of the Red River 119,243
Mount Scott 162,163
Myra (TX) 4,8i,51,170,189-190,191

Natchez (MS) 25,30,31,55
Natchez (Tribe) 20
Natchitoches (LA) 19,20,22,25-
29,34,52,55,63,65,67,68,69,70,72,75,81,92,241,242,
National Auto Trails 79,124,137,212
National Cattle Road 223
New Deal 50,231
Neighbors, Robert 206,207
Newlin (TX) 4,9i,170,233-234
New South 171
New Orleans 25,26,31,55,79,125,184,250

Northrup, Solomon 57,240
North Texas Road 178
Nokona, Peta 228
No man's land 27

Oakland Plantation/Bermuda (LA) 3,5i,54,65-67
Odell (TX) 4,9i,170,224-225
Oil boom 48,54,56,85,195,218,220,221,222,225
Okay (AR) 3,87,106-107,108
Oklahoma Central Railway 138,139
Oklahoma City and Western Railroad 154
Oklahoma Land Rush 142
Old Lady Horse 162,163
"Original 300" 88
Osages 123
Osi Tamaha (OK) 117
Ozan (AR) 3,6i,87,104-105
Ozark Trail 47,154,155

Palo Duro Canyon 9i,14,24,170,205,233,234,236-238
Paraclifta (AR) 13
Parilla, Diego Ortiz 21,193,
Paris 41,176,178
Parker, Cynthia Ann 228-229,
Parker, Quanah 205,228-229
Pecan Point (TX) 30,122,172
Petty (TX) 4,8i,170,177-178
Plains Tribes 20,25,46,204
Platt National Park/Chickasaw Recreational Area 139-140
Porter's Fleet 40
Powhatan (LA) 3,54,68-69
Prairie Dog Town Fork of the Red River 38,230,231,234,236
Preston (TX) 4,8i,36,38,146,170,184-187,194,237
Preston Trail/Cooke's Trail/Preston Road 36,37i,184

Quantrill's Gang 39
Quapaws 123

Ranger (TX) 8i,212,213
range wars 44
Ravenna (TX) 4,8i,170,179-180
Rayburn, Sam 49,50
Reconstruction 41-44,55,103
Red River Crossroads Museum 82,243
Red River Expedition/Custis & Freeman Expedition 27,28,29,94
Red River Landing 55

Red River Meteorite 5i,22,257
Red River rapids 40,241
Red River Station 43,145,194
Red River Valley Museum 224,247
Red River Wars 24,46,151,167,206,214,237
Republic of Texas 30,31,178
Reservation 25,33,40,43,45,46,151,161,169Reed (OK) 4,8i,114,165-166,167,168
Ringgold (TX) 4,8i,170,197-199,200
Rodessa (LA) 3,6i,48,54,85-86
Rondo (AR) 3,6i,30,87,90-91,92
Roosevelt (OK) 4,7i,158-160,161
Roosevelt, Franklin (FDR) 50
Roosevelt, Theodore 159
Rosalie Plantation/Mooreland (LA) 3,54,58-59
Rosedale (OK) 3,7i,114,140-141,142
Rosenwald Schools 107,142,143
Rosenwald Schools 107,142,143

Salt Fork of the Red River 38
San Bernardo 20,21,145,193
San Teodoro 20,21,193,194
Shannon (TX) 4,8i,170,202
Sharecropping 48,49,55,61,63,67,71,72,85
Shawnees 100
Shawnee Trail 36,126,184,245
Sherman (TX) 180,187
Sherman, William Tecumseh 204,214,
Shreve, Henry 34
Shreveport (LA) 34,36,38,43,50,55,56,67,69,71,75,76,80,81,83
Slavery 29,31-32,39,40,57,253
Solomon Northrup Trail 54,57-58,240
Southbend (TX) 4,170,207,208
Southwest Proving Grounds 102
Southwest Trail 88,99,100i,102,104Spanish Louisiana 26-27
Spanish Fort (TX) 4,8i,21,170,192-196,246
Spanish Texas 67,96
Spencer Academy 33,122
Spring Bank Ferry 89,90
Stage Coaches 35,67,76,91,126,127,134,180,203,205
St. Augustine Church 26,64
St. Denis, Louis Juchereau 20
St. Louis and San Francisco Railway 122,159,175
St. Louis and Southwestern Railway/Cottonbelt 92
St. Louis, Iron Mountain and Southern Railway 44,91,104

St. Matthew (LA) 63,54,42,65 Stoneburg (TX) 4,8i,170,198,199-200
Sulphur River 89
Sulphur River Factory 89
Suspension Bridge (TX) 8i,216
Suttenfield, Sophia 185

Tales 'N Trails Museum 197,246
Taovayans 20,21,192,193
Tatums (OK) 3,7i,42,114,140,141-144
Taylortown (LA) 3,6i,54,76-78,79
Texarkana 44,50,90,91,93,95,98,170,245
Texarkana and Fort Smith Railway 110,
Texas and Midland Railroad 178
Texas and Pacific Railway 38,44,45,68,72,83,89,173,176,177,210,211
Texas, Oklahoma and Eastern Railroad 118,119
Texas Rangers 206,228,233
Texas State Bison Herd 236
Texas State Longhorn Herd 215
Texas Trail 36,245
Thalia (TX) 4,9i,170,225-226
Three Forks (Natchez, MS) 30
Thrift (TX) 4,8i,9i,48,170,220-222
Thurber (TX) 4,5i,8i,11,12,170,209-212,213,247
Tishomingo (OK) 126
Tollette (AR) 3,87,107-108
Tone's Bayou 55
Towakonis 20
Trammel Trace 36,88,98,100,102,104
Trail of Tears 116
Treaty of Dancing Rabbit Creek 117
Treaty de San Ildefenso 27
Treaty of San Lorenzo, 26
Trading post 38,54,88,137,145,146,172,185,192,193,194,223,224,241
Turner Falls 136,137-138
Tyson, Charles 83

Ultima Thule 3,32,87,112-113
United Mine Workers 211
US 71 6i,108-109

Valdasta (TX) 4,8i,170,182-183
Vandal, Gilles 83
Victory (OK) 4,7i,114,157-158
Vinson (OK) 4,8i,114,168-169

Walnut Branch Creek 131

Wapanucka Academy 7i,33,133-134
Warren Wagon Train Massacre (Salt Creek Massacre) 214
Washington (AR) 3,6i,30,32,36,45,58,87,91,99-103,104,105,117,240,243
Washita River 50,135,161,186
Webb, Clarence H. 80
West Cache Creek 151
Western Trail/Dodge City Trail 44,215,223,224
Westminster (TX) 4,170,181-182
Wheelock Academy 3,6i,33,114,119-121,122,244
White Oak Shoals (AR) 96
Wichita Agency 34
Wichitas 18,20,22,34,192,206
Wichita, Tillman and Jackson Railway 152
Wichita Falls 50,159,220
Wichita Falls and Hollis Railway 157
Wichita Falls and Northwestern Railway 152,153
Wichita Mountains 161-162,167,227
Wildhorse Creek 222
Wilton (AR) 3,6i,87,108,109-110
Winnipeg (Canada) 79,125
Winthrop (AR) 3,6i,87,111-112
W.K. Gordon Center for Industrial History 247,212
Wolcott, Mary 5,52,
Woodruff, Lt. E.A. 5i,70
Works Progress Administration 160,186
World War I (Great War) 47,48,177,122
World War II 50,101,135,159
Wright's Landing (TX) 172

# *Shameless Self Promotion Page*
www.RedRiverHistorian.com

Initiated in 2001, this non-commercial website has been collecting, documenting, explaining, and sharing the history of the Red River Valley through primary sources, articles, itineraries, and lots of photographs. The website is also the home to Red River Historian Press; museum and preservation consulting; tours of Bonnie and Clyde through Dallas; and presentation bookings, including: The Great Red River Raft, Bonnie and Clyde, Cattle Trails, Hunt for the Red River, Ghost Towns, and Navigation on the Red River.

## Red River Historian Press
- *Traveling History with Bonnie Clyde: A Road Tripper's Guide to Gangster Sites in Middle America*
- *Traveling History along the Cattle Trails: A Road Tripper's Guide to the Cattle Drives of the Southwest*
- *Traveling History among the Ghosts: A Road Tripper's Guide to Abandoned Places in the Red River Valley*
- *Traveling History up the Highways: A Road Tripper's Guide to the Named Roads of the Southwest (coming soon)*
- *The Red River Valley of Arkansas: Gateway to the Southwest (via The History Press)*
- *Images of America: Lewisville, Texas (via Arcadia Publishing)*